Hold My Hand...
It's Dark

James Arthur Hills

Bright Pen

Visit us online at www.authorsonline.co.uk

A Bright Pen Book

Copyright © Darren Storm 2013

Cover design by Corrine McBean ©

British Library Cataloguing in Publication Data.
A catalogue record for this book is available from the British Library.

ISBN 978 0 7552 16062

Authors OnLine Ltd
19 The Cinques
Gamlingay, Sandy
Bedfordshire SG19 3NU
England

This book is also available in e-book format, details of which are available at www.authorsonline.co.uk

In loving memory of
James (Jimmy) Hills

March 1925 – March 2000

Acknowledgements

A big thank you to Helga Hills for her invaluable contribution that helped in the publishing of this book.

Author Summary

James (Jimmy) Hills was born in London on 20 March 1925 and spent much of his early formative years in orphanages and foster homes. It was whilst he was being fostered by a family in East Sussex that he enjoyed the first taste of normal family life with a fine balance of schooling and normal leisure activities such as walking, games and sharing chores. He would come to regard that community and part of England as his home.

He joined the Army in 1943 at the age of 17 (having lied about his real age) and survived till the end of the war when soldiers who joined him, and others met in time, fell around him.

After the war he was posted to barracks near the town of Hanover in preparation for repatriation to England. He met Helga, a young German lady originally from Bochum, got married in Germany and took his bride back to London, where they settled in West London and had two children ; Linda and Ian

Jimmy trained as a gas fitter on his release from the army and helped to rebuild the damaged infrastructures in London. Later he joined the security staff of the South African Embassy, where he worked until his retirement.

Jimmy died on 21 March 2000 and had his ashes strewn over the dales of his beloved East Sussex.

Also by the same author:
The Long Way Home – A moving story about his early life in the orphanages and foster homes *(to be published early 2014)*

Prologue

What makes a man put pen to paper and try to express his thoughts? To me this is a mystery unfathomable. Is it some form of egotism, a desire to create a world of fantasy, of escapism, or, in my own opinion, to put down on paper a thousand and one things he feels, and yet cannot express in words? I make no claims as a literary genius as my educational background does in no way enhance such a claim. In fact, commas, full stops and exclamation marks are to me just the smell of inky classrooms in my youth, and yet I have always felt this strong desire to write.

But then, of what shall I write? Do I create some fictional character, some figment of my imagination, or write just plain facts of the ways of life of ordinary people living their humdrum lives? And in these existences there are enough facts of love, pathos, terror and loneliness to fill a thousand volumes. I choose the latter, because to write of detectives, of sea stories or of history, one's mind must be full of times, dates, clues and a good memory.

In my life I have read only one book the whole way through without cheating, and the writing of Erich Maria Remarque's *All Quiet on the Western Front* left a lasting imprint on my mind. This man, to me, spelt the truth as it should be: stark, realistic and unadorned. His descriptive writing bared the souls of all his characters and left them as they really were: just plain men and women. His chief claim to fame, in my opinion, is the simplicity with which he presents his characters to the ordinary folk like me. No fancy descriptions blot his pages; blood and guts were just that, and it is with an intense admiration for the author that I humbly put my ill-educated pen to paper.

I shall attempt to put the views of the ordinary man of the 1939–1945 war – or shall I say, of mine – across. To me the early part of '39 was of no consequence. I was a boy, just one of millions in those days, carefree and stomach-full. Of course in my mind I did store some of the mutterings of grown-ups about some German named Hitler, of a man named Chamberlain, but to me they were really nothing. A German was the one we shot at playing our games and Chamberlain was a subject for some rude remarks in our childish ways.

1940 came and now it seemed the grown-ups were engaged in some land of war with these Germans. We really did go for this, us kids. Now we thought they really might want us to give them a hand with our wooden guns, our frightening screams and our perambulator tanks. But then it seemed to enter a quiet time, and the words 'Phoney War' was on their lips. This was a great disappointment to us. Our visions of hordes of yelling Jerries faded, and the blood and fury we had so eagerly awaited faded on the horizon of our boyish lives. What was the matter with the grown-ups? We were all sure that we could fight the war ten times better than they could.

There then followed some startling developments. We suddenly found that the usual winners in our playful games were having some awful ill-luck against the Hun, as he was now frequently called by some chap called Churchill.

The years seemed to speed by from this point; the playful children began to join the worried grown-ups and the mantle of responsibility seemed to grow every day. Those boastful cries of childhood were now to be tested on real battlefields against real tanks and guns that splintered your bones, so that the sham fall was not needed.

At this point, I name as a symbol of this generation a youth named John, sturdy of build, of no more intelligence than any more of a million like him. We will follow this boy's entry from here on.

1

The army was John's vocation from 1943. His initial training was hard and rough, and very different from his days of playing soldiers. Here he was driven to the limit of his resources. He went to bed at night with sadness, fear of the unknown that awaited him, thoughts of his mum and dad, and a jumbled mind that can have no description save in those who have actually experienced this. He lay at night wondering whether his friends felt this way too, or whether he was just an outsider in this respect.

The following weeks were full of rumours in the camp: Burma, Italy, a second front. All kinds filled his ears, but no definite word from the 'high-ups'. His best friend was George. They had teamed up soon after his entry into this unit and they shared all the day's gossip together. George was convinced that Italy was their destination, and George was usually right. Anyway, for the time being they were safe and sound in England.

More and more intensive training followed, and boredom began to creep into everybody's minds. Of course there were the sick, the lame and the lazy who were doing everything in their power to work their ticket, but to John and George utter boredom was prevalent. When would

1

the word 'go' be given? Why all this hanging about; surely there was need somewhere? A week, a month, who cared? But someone should give a definite date, after all they were surely first-class soldiers by now. After a further week of rumour upon rumour, a definite statement came in a terse talk from the CO. All he said was that the battalion would be prepared to move, and from then on the barracks became a beehive: trucks, dispatch riders, all the get-up that goes when a fighting unit prepares for action.

John pondered over the prospects of this journey into the unknown. Would his courage fail him in his hour of need? Would he crack up with the sticky fear the old sweats had preached of in those barrack room debates? All these things he knew were shortly to be answered in front of his old friends.

By this time George was practically predicting the landing destination and time of arrival. It was not long before everybody was packed into lorries like sardines and the convoy set off on a journey to a destination they knew not where. After a few hours it was apparent that Liverpool was to be the port of embarkation, and sure enough before long they were pulling into the Gladstone Docks. There, in dock, was a huge trooper lying like some great ark. John's heart felt a huge excitement, a mixture of pride in himself and in his country. Fear, panic, an excitement he had not known before. This was it. The real thing. He looked about him for similar reactions but there was no reading their hearts. Each to his own thoughts. Before he realised where he was going, he was walking up the gangplank into the monster's belly, heavily laden, pack and rifle at a jaunty angle, a thrill in his walk as step by step they disappeared into the black gulf. Curses and shouts of "Where are we going?" rent the air, and John and George were as vehement as the rest. Eventually everybody seemed to be swallowed by this huge creature and their minds were left to ponder as to where she was bound. After what seemed interminable hours, the engines shuddered to life and she headed out of the docks to who knew where. It seemed as if they had been heading out for hours when the klaxon horn sounded for boat drill. Everybody scampered on deck with life jackets on. This in itself gave John a thrill. He thought that this was what it would be like when the real thing came: everybody eager, full of a strange lust to prove himself a man to himself and his comrades.

After the drill he went back to his quarters where the usual card games had started and the company's sex fiend was expounding his theories on the finest ways of lovemaking. John listened avidly to these theories as his own sex life was limited to the timid goodnight kiss, to the hurried embrace of youth. To him this man was crudity itself, yet John was keen to hear more, and gained a yearning for emulating some of the things this man spoke of. He imagined himself in many of the situations this storyteller spoke of and saw himself acquitting himself just as admirably. He listened for hours to the tales that, by this time, were being taken to the uttermost depths of perversion. Did these people actually do the things they boasted of, or were they just trying to impress their sexual prowess on the obvious innocents such as he was?

His worst moment was yet to come when someone called out: "John let's hear about your first bird". He felt his face redden and his tongue stick fast to the roof of his mouth.

He gave a faint grin and just muttered some unintelligible words. They all roared with laughter and someone shouted "he don't know what it's for yet". Others shouted to leave him alone, and for those who joined this chorus he was eternally grateful. Eventually they picked on George, who it seemed was just as depraved as they were. John was really surprised at this, as they had never really talked of sex in their daily gossips, and yet here was George enthralling his audience with his yarns every bit as lurid as those who had taken the platform before him. Anyway, John thought he could boast that he had a mate every bit as versed in the arts as they were. He found quite a satisfaction in this and felt like cheering every time George ended his tales. After this, he would certainly look on George as senior to himself in their friendship. After all, he was obviously a lot more worldly than he was. He suddenly felt a little ashamed at the poor showing he had put up when his first test had been presented, but he thought he would soon be as good as the rest were, and he went over in his mind all the knowledge he had gained in the past few hours. He knew that he would join their ranks when the first woman was made available, but for now, he was safe from this encounter.

Here he was cooped up like a battery hen in some ship bound on an unknown voyage. The days were passed either gazing out onto the huge area of sea all around them or with the card games that abounded in every corner of the ship. The disconsolate faces every now and then signalled another loser. John spent most of his time just staring out into the endless waves in the ship's wake, scanning every horizon for a sight of land, but what did the land hold for him, he wondered. Would he rush off heading into the fray, or would his belly freeze and paralyse his whole being? Would the doctrine of king and country override the sickly fear that makes men at heart just as true as his physical structure will allow? All these things welled up in him in increasing intensity until he felt his brain would flood over.

Relief came as George drew alongside him and asked him whether he felt like a game of crown and anchor, which was fast becoming the vogue on board. Poor old George, who was an eternal optimist imagining his fortune awaiting him just around the corner, invested in a handful of sweating boys in khaki, thought John. Money was the furthest thing from his mind at that moment. Surely George must have a feeling of the unknown such as was with him.

"Hey George", John called, "come and talk a bit". George came closer, rather reluctantly, eager to get away to his gambling. "What's up?" he asked. "You sick or something?"

John smiled. "Christ no", he answered, "don't you ever think of anything but bloody money? No, I just want to speak about where you think we're bound and how and what we're gonna do when we get there."

George's summing up took but a few moments. "It's obvious we're off to Italy to kick the Jerries up the backside in some obscure landing up the coast. It will be a piece of cake and they will scoot like hell when they see this lot."

Good old George! Optimist at cards, optimist in the game of war. But this time his words gave not quite the same reassurance to John as they had done on previous occasions. Also he felt sure, watching his face, that his eyes had the same nervous reaction that he showed when he lost at cards on occasions. So there was a chink in George's armour after all. George was human and probably felt the same as he did, but if he was, he certainly had a better mask to cover his emotions than he had.

"Come on", George said, anxious to scurry off to his maniacal lust for gambling, "there's a fortune going for the asking on A deck – there are a load of old mugs playing brag" and George, according to him, was an invincible bluffer.

"You go", John replied, "I'll stay here for a while. I don't feel like playing. I'll see you later. So long."

Off went George, his eyes alight with anticipation of the lovely loot he would fill his pockets with. John held on to the ship's rails and mused over his thoughts of the past hours. He felt that he was becoming too morbid about it all. Perhaps he should be like George and think of today only and to hell with tomorrow! Who cared, anyway, where they went? He was capable of looking after himself, surely, but in his heart, this stupid outlook found no real resting place.

John forgot time and was brought back to reality by George who had suddenly returned wearing a 'legion of the lost' look. "What's up George?"

The word 'skint' exploded from his mouth. "Them stinking bastards skint me, the thieving pigs. I'd have licked 'em if the game had been straight." He rambled on about his rotten luck until John had to laugh out loud.

"Leave off George, you just lost that's all. Anyway I've got enough for us in the NAAFI. Come on, let's go."

They shuffled off and before long, mugs of steaming char and a couple of the local rock buns had been consumed and simmered George down to talking at normal speed. After they had allowed this meagre bite to find its resting place, they headed off towards the sleeping quarters.

The smell of sweating bodies greeted their nostrils as they stepped inside the packed bunk room. All kinds of humanity were in here, lying about in all forms of dress and undress, frail kids barely navvies, but all in khaki and brought together by the same bits of paper that John had received. He looked round the sea of faces, and in that sea he knew there were the ill-tempered, the kind, the docile, the murderous, the religious and every teeming vice that inhabited the world. A strange silence had now fallen in this place of rest, and save for the boy who played softly on a mouth-organ, it was almost unreal for this usually chattering beehive. George clambered into his bunk, cursing the swaying cot as it swung from side to side. John swung into his quite easily. Soon George was off to the land of Nod. Nothing seemed to disturb him, thought John. On the other hand, sleep never came easily to John. Over the last few days his thinking of anything seemed so confused; everything seemed to be coming after him thick and fast. His mind switched from thought to thought, war, sex, home, mother, father, God, everything jumbled together, twisting, turning, making no real clear picture of today, tomorrow or anything real. Slowly Hypnos blotted

7

out this tortuous picture from his mind, and he joined the rest of this motley company in the only thing in which God had created them equal – sleep.

Night passed, and before John realised it, George was pulling at his blanket. "Come on, rise and shine. Let's have you." He sat up still half asleep and silently cursed the army. Off to the wash-houses, passing steaming bodies rushing to and fro. A gasp as the cold water struck his face. Christ, it was cold straight out of bed! George was a picture of radiance; he seemed to be brimming with zest for living. "Come on, John, let's get first in the breakfast line."

"All right, hang on, let's clean my teeth", said John, "and I'll be with you".

Away they went, scurrying through endless gangways, mess-tins in hand, until they reached mess-deck. A quick scoop of the ladle and a filthy-looking, starchy muck that passed as porridge fell with a plop in the first mess-tin. A jumble of greasy bacon and beans made a sloppy looking panorama in the other one. Some bread, with a heavy mixing of weevils in it, completed the unholy mess that was known by the quartermaster as a 'nourishing meal.' They pushed this filth slowly and methodically into their mouths and belched their way towards their steaming tea mugs to wash it down. "Beautiful", said George. "Don't you want that bread? Give it to me."

By Christ, this boy was like a dustbin, thought John as he pushed the rest of the garbage over to him. They finished their meal and decided to take a stroll on the deck.

There seemed to be a lot of unusual activity by the crew this morning. More ship's officers were seen than usual and a lot more of the 'high-ups' of the crowd were about. By this time, George was beginning to act like Sherlock Holmes. "Hey John, something's going on here. I've an idea we're not far off our destination."

Eleven days had passed, and this in itself was George's main clue, together with the fact that the air seemed warmer than usual on deck and the sea had taken on quite a blue look. By this time, the deck had begun to look like a pleasure steamer. Anxious eyes were scanning everywhere, a buzzing sound of voices of all dialects mingled together, Tyke, Scot, Lancastrian, Welsh, English, Irish, the heart-warming sounds of your fellow countrymen that gave you the feeling of not being alone.

"It's land. I can see it". The shout came from an obvious Yorky. A thousand eyes followed his quivering hand. "There, over there". John's eyes flashed in the direction pointed out, and sure enough it was. His whole body started tingling with excitement. George was roaring a triumphant 'I told you.' The rest of the boys seemed to be hypnotised by the sight of the coastline.

"Where is it, George?" John asked.

"I've told you a thousand times", he half shouted. "Italy. I feel I'm right. You'll see." But there was a long time sailing before they would know for sure, he said.

A long time. It seemed years to John, but slowly the coastline drew nearer and nearer. Murmurs of 'Naples' were spreading fast. The prophets were correct. Soon picture-card Naples was on top of them. "See Naples and die", thought John. Were these words meant in a sinister way, or just for the sheer beauty that lay before his eyes at this moment? Naples, shimmering in the heat, of magnificent surroundings, the bay a gem set in a ring of gold, the careworn faces of Italians wreathed in smiles of welcome as the great ship weaved its way to berth after its tiring journey – a monster in need of food for its engines – a truly trustworthy and faithful ark.

Hours had passed and the boys had all been ushered off the ship and settled on some wasteland not far out of the dock area. John surveyed the scene around him. So, this is Italy. That land of the Roman conquerors he had read about in books. Home of Julius Caesar and ice-cream. At least as far as Italy went, John's knowledge was extremely limited to pure, basic fact. George was quickly by his side, boasting to high heavens about his clairvoyant powers of predicting their ultimate destination.

"Okay George, you were right", said John. "What do you want, a special medal struck?"

By now, the whole rigmarole of packing the boys in trucks was starting again, and before long they were jogging along dusty roads in convoy. John, his eyes skimming around for sight of these Romans, took everything in from the view at the back of the truck. They waved at everybody they passed and wolf-whistled even women of 70 at least. The boys all seemed in quite a gleeful mood and began to sing. Anything that came to mind. All the old stuff: 'Roll out the Barrel', 'Nellie Dean', all the old faithful songs the British roll out when adversity appears to be their lot.

The trucks wound their way on and presently began to head towards a small village some way outside Naples itself. Military police motorcyclists began to show the leading truck the way in, and George suddenly said: "Good, it's not too far from Naples itself. We'll be able to go into the city and sort out some of the Eyetie women." Good old George! Here they were, just landed in a foreign land, all the beauty, all the mystery, all the strangeness, and George could only think of his lust for the women. But still, John always felt safe when George was around. He looked on this ape as his own brother, and when George was glad, happy or sad, John's moods seemed to run in unison.

Hours passed in settlement of the boys in rows of Nissen huts; with the latrine-digging squad in action at full speed, cooks rushing about organising their slops and sergeant majors roaring their tonsils out, the camp slowly began to take on signs of habitation. John and George were now settled in and congratulating themselves on having escaped some of the more arduous tasks the others had been caught up for.

"Come and get it", the old cry went up, and off they went for the first meal in their new surroundings. It turned out to be the old standby, Maconochie Stew. Still, it tasted good for once, even if only for the fact that it was eaten on land. After the meal was over, a few more orders were issued and the rest of the day passed uneventfully. As night drew on, John went outside the hut and gazed up at the sky to stars that he had looked at millions of times in England. The world was not as big as he had imagined. God looked down here just as he did at home, only the air was warmer and the people darker-skinned. Life went on

11

here with just the same intensity as anywhere else. There were just the same ingredients: anger, jealousy, tenderness, hatred. These people lived and died just the same way, the cemeteries filled as at home. He fell silent in mind for a few moments, and then went back inside. George was stretched out in his birthday suit on the bunk, eyes half-closed.

"Come on, John, you silly bastard. Get in kip. We'll sort this place out in the morning."

"Yeah sure", said John. "Goodnight George." He just grunted and was out to the world. Yes, tomorrow, thought John. We'll see. And before long, he too dozed off.

2

Morning came and there was intense activity, most of the time in organising the companies to be placed under the commands of various officers. John and George were placed in the same company and at this John was greatly relieved. He hated the thought of being without his mate in whom he placed great faith. Their commanding officer was one of the more popular types with the boys; a Scot who had the reputation of being no fool, but a fair-minded man. Later in the afternoon he called his men together in the recreation hut and addressed them as 'A Company', as they were now to be termed. He spoke of the need for a good showing on their part and all the usual patter that goes in an address of this type. His main warning came about their need for strict observance of their behaviour towards the civilian population; this, he stressed, would be closely watched, and any man found guilty of any complaints would be heavily punished. They were to be allowed out from that night until further orders. He closed his speech with a wink, followed by the words: "And watch your step with the local maidens." A roar of laughter and wolf-whistles greeted this remark and the boys dispersed to their various huts. George walked alongside John, rubbing his hands together and almost leering. "Let's go and get togged up and get downtown", he said. "I'll find out when the trucks are leaving."

"Okay", said John. He felt, too, that they should see what Naples held for them.

George scurried off and John headed towards their hut. Before long they were both dressed to kill and on their way into Naples. On arrival they made straight for the first place that looked like a bar. It was scruffy-looking inside, and they were greeted by a rather stout dark-haired woman in her fifties. "Yes, Johnnie", she said, "you want vino?" It seemed that all the British were known as 'Johnnie' out here, as she addressed some of the other boys with the same introduction. John said yes, not even knowing what this strange-sounding stuff tasted like. A bottle was thrust in front of them and they filled their two rather dirty-looking glasses to the brim, trying to look like two hardened drinkers. They raised and clinked glasses with a 'down the hatch' exclamation. John winced as he took a large gulp. It was vile, he thought, just like vinegar. George, it seemed, could drink ditch water without the slightest facial expression.

"It's good", he said, "here, fill up".

John again put up an act and somehow managed to empty his glass again. The old woman came over and after a few moments began to mention that she had a bottle of vermouth, apparently noticing John's pained expression.

"Yes", said George, "bring that. It all goes down the same way"

An hour passed. To John the vermouth was infinitely better tasting than the wretched vino, and his cheeks had now taken on a reddish glow. He also felt quite talkative and bolder in spirit than usual. They sat there, running down sergeants and officers in general until George said: "Let's go and find a couple of birds." After paying out a fortune in paper lira, they crept back out into the street feeling quite merry. The streets, they found, were quite narrow, and rather poor-looking civilians eyed their steps as they walked slowly up and down each street they came across.

Suddenly, from a doorway, a hiss and a voice: "Hello boys. You want girls?"

George almost ran over to the voice. He made no bones about it. "How much?" he asked. By this time they found that the voice belonged to a rather oily-looking character who introduced himself as Tony.

"You got cigarettes, tobacco?"

"Only 20", said George. "My friend's got 20 as well." He winked broadly at John.

"Okay", said Tony, "upstairs".

They climbed a dingy set of stairs to a filthy room at the top, and waited in there while Tony went into another room further along the hall. Presently he returned and motioned them to follow him. At the end of the hall they entered a room with a dim lamp and could just make out two women sitting across a bed at the far end, both scantily dressed, with the marks of their occupation written in years on their faces. By this time, George had almost leapt across the room towards the plumper of the two and began to act like a young Rudolph Valentino. "Come on John", he shouted, "grab hold of the other bird".

John's face began to burn. The woman walked over to him, gave a laugh and rattled off in Italian, ending with the word 'bambino'. This was one of the few words John understood and his senses told him that this woman was mocking his youth. His awful embarrassment grew as she took his arm and pulled him towards the large bed, which apparently both women shared. In the meantime, George was partially undressed and the other woman practically naked. John wished at that moment that the floor would open up and swallow him. Surely this would not be his introduction to sex. But he felt he could not back out now, although his every movement was one of reluctance. George, he thought, was a real filthy bastard. Fancy, right in front of him. Did he really not mind his being there, or was this just showing off his experience with the birds?

John was now lying on the same bed as these two filthy pigs and was slowly surrendering the last vestige of decency he felt he had ever had. The woman's faint whisperings, although in Italian, were unmistakably the same words whispered by women in other parts of the globe, and John's clumsy fumblings stood out to her as clearly as a choirboy's. He glanced, embarrassed, at George, and made feeble attempts to copy, but the whole mad set up was so unreal that he thought it a nightmare. His whole body shuddered as his childlike passion was expended, and he lay there tired and with a feeling of absolute disgust at the bitch who lay beside him. It was peculiar, even to John, that just for a few fleeting seconds this woman seemed to be the most beautiful creature on God's earth. Yet here she lay now, seemingly unaware that he was there, and he hated her guts. He could have willingly killed her seconds after. The filthy cow, he thought.

He jumped up off the bed and hurriedly put his trousers back on, hiding himself from her gaze as much as possible, although he knew she had seen a thousand like him. By this time George was oblivious to everything and everyone in the world, and John was at a loss for the moment as to what to do or where to go. Eventually he tossed 20 cigarettes at his bed companion and strode off out of the room. Tony was waiting at the end of the hall. "Okay, Johnnie. You like?" John tried his hardest to look nonchalant and just said: "Yeah, not bad." But he knew Tony was not deceived by it, and was sure he saw the look of fleeting pity in his eyes.

John almost ran out into the street to gulp down some fresh air. He felt somehow dirty in mind and body, and a feeling of having committed some crime of enormity, and yet this was not illegal (most of the boys would have given their right arms to have been in his position ten minutes previously). He lit a cigarette and wondered what the hell George was up to. Surely he had finished with that old tom by now. By Christ, that filthy old git didn't care who watched, he laughed quietly to himself.

Minutes later, George staggered out doing up his buttons and roaring with laughter. "What an old scrubber", he said. "She was old enough to be my granny. Still, not too bad."

John gave him a searching look. "You took your time; what kept you?"

George grabbed him by the arm and with a confidential wink said: "You gotta learn to control yourself son. Not like you – on and off."

John felt his face redden again. So, George had also noticed that he was a new boy at the game. Still, it was experience and the next time, perhaps, he would not feel such a mug. They walked off slowly down the street, John by this time trying to copy the swaggering walk his mate always adopted, and feeling quite an old veteran of the brothels.

"Now, did you like it John?" George asked.

"Not bad", John replied, "but she wasn't my type". This was an excuse he had brought in at the spur of the moment to cover his poor showing, but George seemed not to notice.

"They are all the same in bed. You'll see, the next one will be just the same," he said. "They love me because I satisfy them. You'll learn as time goes on."

John felt smaller than he had ever felt before. George must have seen the performance he had made, and here he was gently chiding him for it. He tried to change the subject. "How about something to eat?" he said. George muttered something about the Eyeties all starving themselves and said: "Let's get back to camp, I'm tired." John was grateful for this remark. He could think of nothing better at that moment than lying in bed and being alone with his thoughts of the day that was surely to be a milestone in his life.

Back at camp, some of the others had returned and were telling of their adventures in town. George related his yarn, and whether out of pity or good nature, did not include John's performance in his story. A great relief had swept over him for this omission, as the majority of the boys would be only too delighted to take the mickey out of anyone who did not conform to some of their perverted standards. George now appeared to have forgotten his tiredness and was revelling in some yarn one of the boys was spilling. It seemed that two of them had spent their evening with a couple of birds in a single bed and the performance put up by them was little short of hilarious. At least, thought John, theirs had been a double bed and there was a slight space for manoeuvre, although at the time it had seemed the smallest bed in the world in which to indulge in sexual activities of any kind. It gave John a feeling of embarrassment just to think back to it. Never mind, it was over now, but he felt sure the next time he would acquit himself in a more adequate manner. Yes, the next time. But how many chances for the next time were there to be? How long would they remain in this village? After all, the war was the primary reason they were here, and as pawns in this huge game they could be switched at a moment's notice. This was no holiday camp, he thought, it was a camp full of legally trained killers who would be eventually asked to slaughter their fellow men, to maim and kill those of a different coloured uniform, because their governments could not see eye to eye. It was as simple as that. He did not know these men, but he had been taught to hate them. Throughout his whole training session, even bayonet drill, he had been told to scream out as he lunged at a straw-filled sack dressed as his adversary. Still, his was not to reason why, but to do or die. And yet, somehow, these words seemed to him to be made by someone higher up as an excuse, to make one such as he do something entirely foreign to his normal nature.

But enough of this philosophising, he thought. Those who thought too deeply on subjects of this nature were generally viewed with a certain amount of suspicion by the officers who regarded them somewhat as mischief makers and alarmists, and fellows who did not have pride in the Empire and the tradition the British had built the world over.

John flopped into bed and slowly began to run over the day's events in his mind. What a mess he had made with that woman, he thought. She must have laughed her head off when he left. At least he was not there to hear it. He rambled on through event after event, until sleep eventually cloaked his mind with its healing balm.

3

The next day arrived and the one after, and weeks appeared to fly by. They went into town and John, by this time, was learning fast with the girls and was now beginning to really relish his excursions. George now seemed to be treating him a little more like an equal at the bird game, too.

They were in Naples and on the eternal scout around for talent when John spotted her. She stood in the doorway of a rather poor-looking house. Her hair was long and black, she wore a simple dress and her feet were bare. George had also spotted her and was rapidly making strides in her direction. "Leave her", said John sharply.

George stared at him for a moment, then he smiled. "Okay" he said, "we'll toss a coin. Heads or tails?"

"No" said John. Somehow he felt this was not right. "Please George, let me have this one. I'll see you later."

George grinned broadly. "All right, John", he said. "There's plenty more fish in the sea. She's yours. I'll see you back at camp."

John wandered off in the direction of the girl and clumsily walked up to her. "Hello," he said.

She ignored him, turning her head in the opposite direction from his gaze. John was flummoxed by this. "You speak English?", he enquired. This always worked in situations like this as an opening gambit, and she turned towards him.

"Yes, a little," she answered coldly.

Her face was lovely, thought John, although he could see she was no pick-up by her manner, and for once he was glad she wasn't. Here was a thing of beauty and someone, he felt, that was a class above some of the bags he'd been used to associating with lately. Awkwardly, he tried to move a little closer to her, but she backed away into the doorway.

"What do you want?" she asked. "I not soldiers' lady. Please you go away."
"No please," said John. "I know you're not. I just want someone to talk to, that's all, honest."

She seemed to relax a little at this, and came back to her original position in the doorway.

"You live here?" he asked, motioning beyond the doorway.

"Yes," she replied. "This is my house." She smiled lightly and John noticed the perfect set of teeth that came through her pretty lips.

"And your parents?" he enquired.

"Just Momma. Poppa dead." She stopped smiling and a serious look took over.

John felt a wave of sympathy sweep over him. She was so young and appeared to be so innocent, and he was glad he had not risked tossing the coin. The thought of what George could have done to this kid made him feel almost sick.

They made small talk for another half an hour or so and as time went on, the girl smiled a lot more than before. She seemed to be losing some of the mistrust she had had for John, and through signs and half-English, and the smattering of Italian John had been able to learn, they had quite a conversation.

It was starting to get late, and John felt that the evening was far too short; he wished he could create time to stay and talk more with this girl.

"I must go now." She smiled at his disappointed gestures. "Maybe I could come and see you again?"

"Yes, if you want," she stated simply.

"Tomorrow then?" John searched her face eagerly, hoping she would agree and his hopes were rewarded.

"Okay, tomorrow."

"Same place, same time?" He half lifted his arm to put it around her shoulders and kiss her, but then dropped it again quickly. This might frighten her off, he thought, and he didn't want that to happen. A quick turn and he strode off, constantly stopping to wave back until she was out of view.

She faded out of sight but not out of mind. As he made his way along the narrow streets, her face was an image constantly before him. She was vastly different this one: tender, with a more true-eyed appearance than the others. He recalled the number of street jockeys he had made love to and kissed goodbye. Old scrubbers, the majority of them, who thought no more of him than he thought of them, but this girl he felt he must see again. Was this the start of that soppy condition 'love' that the boys all derided? Perhaps she had more guile that the rest of the pack and was now laughing at the silly little Englishman. But he quickly dispelled these thoughts, because in his heart he wanted to.

This girl was something he wanted to keep just for himself. In his mind he began to place her on a pedestal of sheer purity and any dirty images became intruders into his imagination. He knew when he returned to camp what George's first words would be: 'did you or didn't you?'. A stock phrase in his repertoire of filth. Somehow the very thought of this became repugnant to him. He felt the blood rushing to his head. He would let George know that this one was something special, someone he had not attempted to maul, and whom he liked to think of as a virgin, even if only in his heart this were true. He was comforted by the feeling that he would see her again soon and the next day would seem endless. He laughed quietly to himself. Here he was, placing this girl in that category and he had not even asked her name. But he would put that right when next they met. I suppose it's Maria, he thought; everyone seemed to be a Maria in the female line, but who cared? What's in a name? It's the person that counts, even people with the double-barrelled ones were guilty of the sins of the lesser classes. Some of his officers really displayed their true breeding when the drink was flashing about.

Before he realised it, he was back at camp and walking in to his hut. John looked around for George. No sign of him yet. I suppose he's teamed up with an old slag somewhere and perhaps going to kip out for the night and chance his arm getting back in the early hours of the morning. This was quite a common practice with some of the boys, but the penalties were rather severe if they were caught. John began to undress, throwing his clothes all over the place much against his soldierly grain. Somehow he did not care much about the army that night, his thoughts were centred on the girl he had been with hours before. He clambered into his bed and lay back with his arms behind his head on the pillow. She loomed in front of his eyes, conjured there by his imagination. He began to think of all the things he could have said to her and had not. He cursed silently the time he had wasted muttering nonsense just for the sake of keeping her in conversation. Now he could think clearly of sensible things to say and his nerves were as steady as a rock. But while she had been with him he had been a bundle of nerves.

His senses were suddenly brought crashing back to reality by a loud singing voice lustily heading toward his hut and unmistakably being that of George. The hut door flew open and there before his eyes was his old pal covered in dust, one eye appearing to swell rapidly, a bloodied mouth and battledress jacket draped over his arm. "Hello my old son!" This greeting to John was a sure sign that the ape-man was stinking rotten drunk. Before he had time to reply, the burly one was beginning to explain the reasons for his startling and unkempt appearance. "You see", said George, "there was this little bird down the street, and this guardsman geezer and me spots her at the same time, but I got to her first and was just presenting my credentials when he decided to question the validity of them." During this outburst, George was dancing quite a good tango and seemed to have difficulty deciding between floor and ceiling. Mixed up with beery belches and much arm waving, he began to appear more like a puppet than a person. He rambled on: "I smacked him one, and we settled the difference there and then."

John smiled. "And I suppose you won."

"Well", George said, "not exactly, because he smacked me one back and while I was getting over it, he scarpered with the bird. But I'll know his face again." And then with a flow of eloquence John had never heard him express before, he began to explain the dire peril this soldier would be in if he ever crossed George's path again. He suddenly seemed to fall short of words and sat staring moodily in front of him. After a pause in which John tried to console him, urging him to wash the blood from his mouth and clean up his suit a bit, George asked: "Anyhow, how did you get on with that bit of skirt I left you with?"

John's face coloured up. "All right," he said, half fearing what was coming next. He knew the inevitable question would be asked, and yet he felt this burning resentment boiling up inside him.

George grinned like an Alsatian bearing its teeth. "Come on, Johnnie, tell your old mate. Was she all right?" John sat bolt upright in bed.

"Mind your own bloody business, you filthy bastard. Can't a man have any decent ways in him?"

George stared at John for a moment, completely taken aback by this outburst. "What's up with you now? You in love or something? Come off it, you're acting like an overgrown schoolboy. You can't go falling for every pretty face you see 'cos you'll end up having hundreds of the silly cows all round you."

John could see that he had not understood his feelings, and began to pity this huge fellow, and at the same time envy him for the shield he possessed, that he, John, did not have. "No, it's not that, George, but you always think that's all there is to a girl. Can't you ever see anything else?"

George gave a half-doped grin. "Not the ones I go out with. They know what I'm after and if they don't cooperate, I sling 'em and look for someone else who will," he said simply.

"Yes, but you must surely at one time have liked a girl so much that you felt she was someone you would have liked to marry?" John put this question in the simplest way he could think of, as he knew George's brain was limited to the apparently childish questions or crude ones of the moment.

"Yes, there was a girl once, down the bottom of our road. She was a little cracker, and my Mum always used to say that I would be alright if I got hitched up with her. But her old man hated my guts 'cos I did a stretch in borstal, so she went and got herself a posh bloke out of an office and I ain't seen her since." Poor old George, a genuine look of sadness clouded his face, and John, for a moment, felt very sorry he had probed into George's private affairs. Perhaps this man had an inner sadness that he could not understand. Maybe in this one small, trivial slice of life, he had suffered pain and humiliation that had cut through even his thick hide. How much this had hurt him, who knew. Only George had the key.

"Never mind George, there are others," John said. "You'll come across one, someday, just as good as her, who won't care what you did in the past and see you only as yourself."

George just shrugged his shoulders. "I don't care anyway. I'm enjoying myself as it is without all that marriage trash."

John felt it was wise to leave it at that as it was getting late and he did not fancy a long session of George's alcoholic philosophising. "Goodnight, George. Give us a shout in the morning if I don't hear old 'guts-ache' call us."

"Sure", George said, as he wearily kicked off his boots and slowly undressed. "We have got to listen to that old sky pilot giving us a lecture in the morning." This was his favourite name for the padre, and George usually voted his religious denomination to the sect who gained the least fatigue duties.

The two comrades were well asleep before the rest of the occupants of the hut returned, and morning came, as usual, much too early. The morning was quite crisp until the sun came up, and they busied themselves with their duties with a gusto not to be found in them later in the day.

"Coming out tonight John?" George looked expectantly at him, confident of an affirmative reply.

"No George, I'm going on my own tonight and seeing the one I saw last night." John even felt guilty calling her 'the one', but he consoled himself with the fact that tonight he would at least know her name.

George gave him a sour look. "Christ, that bird has sure got you by the tail. Why don't you put in the banns?"

"Forget it", said John, "you go your way and I'll go mine".

But to the immediate and present future – a corporal was rushing them towards a large Nissen hut where God's emissary on earth awaited the salvation of their souls. They filed in, some openly bored, some with reverence shining in their faces. John took his place and pondered as to what religion meant to him.

He had done the ordinary round of Sunday schools as a child and had listened in awe to some of the local preacher's threats of hell, but as it stood in his own mind at present, there were lots of gaps to be filled in. He kept a more or less open mind on the subject of God, a fear to blaspheme, and yet ready to scoff with the rest if need be, as an undecided Judas. George, he knew for a fact, thought as much about religion as he did of the company cook, and for him this would be a painful session. It would only give him an opportunity of thinking over his impending nocturnal operations.

The padre arrived and began to lecture them on a dozen or so themes. Not like the civvy preachers this one, thought John. They gave you the full fire and brimstone treatment. This one just more or less substantiated the officer's warnings about behaviour, throwing in a few bits about Jesus here and there and ending up with a good solid 'Amen' every now and again. John tried to look interested but found his mind wandering towards his night out. George just sat blatantly picking his nose and staring at a fly making its way up the chair back ahead of him. After some weak godly jokes that the boys in the barracks would have yawned at, the preacher gave them relief by letting the boys out of the hut. As soon as the rush was over and George's fly had made a hurried departure from the quickly moving throng, they scooted quickly across to their own hut to grab their mess tins and once more suffer the wrath of the Lord in the unholy mess served up as the midday meal.

"Not a bad old stick, that geezer," said George. "I suppose he means well, but he would drive me round the bend if I had to listen to him for long. I wonder what his old woman thinks when he leads off like that."

"Perhaps he's not married," John replied.

"No, I don't suppose he is. Them old vicars usually have a bit on the side," George grinned. "They're right artful old souls really." George could be the devil's right-hand man, thought John, the way he carried out his preachings, but John often wondered on what boss George would call when the chips were really down.

The afternoon seemed to drag and they were caught for one or two fatigue duties not usually on their programme. Eventually the time came to get out for night manoeuvres, as George termed them. They were both now in the middle of their preparations, cleaning their boots, polishing their cap badges and the host of small items to boost a man's peacock image. George gazed in the mirror and swore that there was none so fair. John felt himself taking more time than usual and extra special care in his personal appearance. Having completed their toilet operations, they proceeded out of camp towards town.

"So I won't be seeing you once we get there?" George asked.

"Sorry", replied John, "not tonight; perhaps tomorrow." He knew as he said this that it was false, because if all went well, he would see this girl on his own at every opportunity.

"Okay," George stated. "Good luck John, and don't forget…" He was about to say something but suddenly stopped, gave a big grin and looked heavenward.

They soon arrived in town and, with a wave, parted on their different paths. George no doubt to the nearest vino shed to some 'old bag' he would cheat with some outrageous story about his once being a captain or something to that effect. John, on the other hand, had his opening speech all laid out in his mind, and yet he wondered whether he would be able to say it all when he met this girl. He was not far from their meeting place when his heart began to beat faster, his feet hurried along and with a few yards around the corner left, he adjusted his tie again. Would she be there? He would know in a few seconds. Before he realised it, she was in view, waiting in the doorway he had seen in his visions during the previous hours. He began to slow his pace a little; he did not want her to see him like some eager kid at a Sunday school outing. No, he would try to give her the man-of-the-world look. "Hello", he said simply, "been here long?" His opening speech had already been forgotten.

She smiled: "Not long I wait, maybe four minutes."

"By the way, what's your name? I forgot to ask you last night."

"Rita", she said, "and you?"

John felt himself blush a little. "John," he replied. It was funny, but he always felt a little awkward telling people his name.

"That's nice", she informed him, "I like your name."

"Oh. Yours too", and he felt like kicking himself for not having given her the compliment when first she had told him her name.

"How old are you?" John asked rather suddenly. 'Seventeen? Eighteen?" He began to hold his fingers up.

She laughed. "It's okay. I can understand you. I am seventeen."

"Oh, you're quite young." John felt he was getting tongue-tied. He was desperately searching about for words with which to make conversation. Rita was cool while he was reaching boiling point and they had only been together for a few minutes. She looked at him and John sensed that she knew the dilemma he was faced with.

"Where's your big friend from yesterday?"

"Oh, him." He's not my friend, just a man I know from the camp." 'Judas' he condemned himself inwardly. After all, George was truly his pal, and here he stood denying him outright. "You look pretty tonight, Rita." He said. It was the first time he had used her name and the way he said it made her smile.

"You tell all the ladies same?" she asked.

"No, that's not true," he retorted quickly. The conversation seemed similar to his boyhood days when he had taken little Shirley out from the house next door and they had whispered all this childish nonsense. His mind began to tick over furiously: should he suddenly seize her and give her the 'cave-man' approach, or string along with the adolescent clap-trap that usually ended with a timid goodnight kiss after hours of feather-preening? The former policy, he feared, would only frighten this lovely creature away from him, and he also feared his own ability to stage-manage the situation. The latter approach, for now, seemed the only way open to him, but he longed to be more masterful in effect than he was at present.

"Honest," he said. "I haven't taken many girls out like you. Well, you know what I mean."

She blushed slightly, perhaps sensing a compliment, or that she was perhaps not versed enough in the ways of the world for him. Suddenly John put an arm round her shoulders; his hand resting gently on her trembled and she must have felt this. Rita stayed propped against the door and John felt a wave of relief that she had not panicked and run inside. She was closer to him now than she had ever been and John could smell her freshly washed hair and slight perfume she wore. She looked up at him and smiled.

"Are you frightened of me, John?"

"Why should I be?" he enquired, trying to keep his hand steady on her shoulder.

"Because your hand shakes," she replied simply.

"Oh that! Well, you know, I thought you might run away."

"Why should I? You do nothing wrong."

God, this girl could put the most awkward answers into the most awkward places. She laughed out loud when she saw his blushing face.

"Perhaps you would like to go for a walk somewhere?" This was one question John entirely agreed with as his arm was killing him, holding it around her, yet it would have taken a surgical operation to make him remove it.

"Sure let's go."

As she moved from the doorway, John slowly dropped his arm till it was around her slim waist and they moved off down the road. They talked on one subject and then another, and John was amazed at how much English the girl knew. By that time he felt she was warming to him, and now and again she laid her head on his shoulder. Inquisitive Italians eyed them up and down as they passed and some even looked disgusted, but John saw only Rita by his side. Eventually they stopped at the side of an old farm. She leaned against the door of a barn and John was forced to take his arm away from around her waist. He quickly put both his hands on her shoulders and slowly bent forward to kiss her. She pressed her lips closely to his and held on to him for a few seconds.

"So you're not such a bambino after all," she said. The word 'bambino' stung John. He had come to hate the word. It reminded him of the wretched episode at Tony's.

"Don't say that word, Rita", John said sharply.

"Why? You not like?"

"Oh, it's nothing, it just reminds me of something unpleasant, that's all."

She looked slightly hurt, but he pressed her closer to him and kissed her again, this time more fervently than the previous time. John could feel his passions for this girl rising stronger as they remained locked in embrace and Rita seemed to see the red light. She broke away from John and smiled teasingly.

"How many girls you kiss like that, John?" He was at a loss for the moment as to how to reply. He could only think clearly of the desire in him to kiss this girl again and again.

"Rita, I want you to be my girl for always," he said softly. "I have kissed others, but they were not like you, and I don't want to tell you about them as they are of no interest any more."

"You're a funny boy, John. You meet plenty girls better than me in England one day, and you forget all about me. Maybe it's because you not at home now."

"No, Rita, it's not true. I want someone like you to call my own." John now felt the need to tell this girl he was falling in love with her. Even if this be infatuation, he hoped it would go on for ever and ever. He felt a need to cling to her, to shut out the rest of the world around him, and to hold her in his arms and tell her that no one would ever take her place. He pulled her close to him again. "Say it, Rita, say it's just you and me."

"All right, John, I'll be your girl."

He pulled her fiercely to him. "I love you, Rita. I promise you're the only one for me." He kissed her again and again, and this time John felt Rita's embrace to be more passionate and intense.

"I love you too, John. Please not make a fool of me. I only want you now and I'll be your girl always."

The words were just what John wanted to hear and for the next few minutes they were in a world known only to the young at heart. Their kisses cascaded one after the other and the joy of living and loving soared like a lark in flight on a spring morning. Eventually, with their arms around each other, they moved on back towards Rita's house as the evening, for John, was coming to a close. To him it had seemed just a moment in time, and yet hours had passed; he realised he was now was the possessor of something that, to him, was greater than the wealth of the richest person in the world. A love he felt would surmount all obstacles that this stinking world could throw in its path. He had only known this girl for two nights and yet here she was now, more precious to him than the jewels of the Orient. Something clean and pure, someone never to be soiled by the George's of this world, someone that would for ever be warm and tender and love him, only. It was a warm feeling and one that made his walk seem lighter and his whole being flooded with a new zest for life. Let this be for always, never let this moment in time move on. Let Rita be at his side as she was now, and the whole world carry on marching along. But leave them behind with just their little share of happiness. Their love for each other would shine out through the darkest hours. Their kisses tonight sealed two lonely youngsters' hearts with a love that would last till eternity, and John was grateful to be alive and to know that a bond of affection born of their meeting on this night would flourish forever.

They came nearer now to Rita's house and their arms gripped each other tighter, as though this was to be farewell. But no, with a reassuring look, John began to plan tomorrow night's meeting.

"I'll see you same place, darling. It won't be long and I'll be back."

She trembled slightly and held on to him. "You come for sure, John? I believe you. I'll always love you, and the day will soon pass."

They were now at Rita's front door. He took her in his arms and her tears began to flow and a lump came into his own throat. They held each other for a last moment, a final goodnight kiss sealed a tremendous day in John's life. This had been a day in which he had learned that there existed a feeling of true love not to be found in any street-woman's bed. A last press of hands and he was off, heading back towards camp, wishing the very minutes to hasten away and bring tomorrow's night. The last truck would have gone by now, but he would walk under the blanket of stars and just run over in his mind the tender moments they had shared this night. With her words "I love you, John" ringing clearly in his ears, it was not long before he reached camp. He walked past the sentry who rapidly put out the cigarette he had been craftily smoking, and with a cheery "goodnight" walked over to his hut.

Some of the boys who had stayed in looked up. "Hello John boy, had a good time?" asked Mac, the Scot lad.

"Yes, great," answered John with a smile.

"Good", stated Mac, "I hope you said goodbye, or have you not heard we're on the move tomorrow?"

John's mind could not grasp the significance of those last words. "How do you mean, on the move?"

"We're away, Johnnie boy, to help some of the field-marshals to keep their batons."

John's whole being froze. Please God let this not be true, let this be a joke they were playing on him. Not now, please, not now. His mind went into torment and his face must have betrayed his emotions, for Mac suddenly said, "Don't take it like that, son. We all knew it had to come one day." But Mac did not know how he felt just now. Nothing could help him at this moment, neither God, nor fellow man. John looked dazedly over to the voice that had dealt this hurtful blow.

"When? What time? Do you know?"

"Sometime before midday," Mac said quietly, sensing that this was important to the youngster who stood before him. John could not even raise a thanks, his guts were twisted and he felt sick. Sometime before midday! "Oh my God, Rita, I'll always love you." He hurried over to his bed and faced the wall, ashamed to let the other boys see the tears that had welled up in his eyes. What could he do? Where did man turn to in a moment such as this? Who could heal this deadly wound? His mind could find no answer. Her words "I believe you John" hurt him the most now, and yet when she had said them they had been music to his ears. "I'll be your girl." It all came to him in a ghostly chorus. Was this to be the way he would leave her, with no word, no tiny note? Was she to remember him as an Englishman who whispered sweet-nothings to her just to pass the night away? What a mess; what a rotten, dirty stinking mess! He felt a stinging resentment rise within him toward the army and everyone in authority in general, and with the realisation that he was but a tiny cog in this huge mass of humanity that governments welded into armies. As far as he was concerned at this moment, the

German army could take the whole of Italy and keep it, as long as they left him his little piece of happiness.

George came in, hardly noticed by John until he sat on the end of his bed. "I suppose you have heard, my old son?" Even George could see he had, by the abject look of misery on his face. "Well that's it," he continued. "My old darlings are all going to miss me, they sure are."

John stared at him. If only he could dismiss that girl as George did his. If only he had the same feelings this man had and could brush off Rita as just another bird on life's road, but he knew, try as he may, this could never be. He began to feel a little calmer now as the initial shock of the news had subsided. His only thought now was how to get word to Rita that he could not keep their date and to make some kind of arrangement to keep in touch. There was only one way: he must skip out of camp some time between now and midday tomorrow and let her know, and there was no time like the present. But what if she were asleep and he woke the whole neighbourhood up? Who cared?, he thought, this was something greater to him than anything else.

He called softly to George. "I'm going to break away from camp for a couple of hours. Cover me if you can."

"Okay, you must have something bad, my old son. Is it the bird you have been hibernating with lately?"

John just nodded. "I won't be long. Try to cover me."

He ran over to the door and in a flash was heading for the hole in the barbed wire that the boys had made for the purpose of the night-outers and nick-named 'escape route'. It was soon reached, and on hands and knees he began to crawl under it. All of a sudden he stopped crawling, holding his position static like a pointer dog. There, unmistakably, was a pair of white gaiters and a white belt standing only a foot from the wire. They stood out a mile in the darkness and John knew they were wrapped round one of the military police. He knew that his last avenue of escape was now denied him and desperation took over. White gaiters had seen him and he must move fast. He backed quickly into the camp's boundaries and fled headlong towards his hut, not stopping to see whether his pursuer was on his heels. He burst through the hut door and dived fully clothed into bed. Half the boys sat up quickly. "What's up?" they chorused.

"Redcaps!" John replied urgently.

Everyone lay back down as the door flew open. Framed in the doorway stood White Gaiters. He paused, and John, peeping through half-closed eyes, saw his gaze go from bed to bed. After an age, he about turned and left as quickly as he had come in, no doubt to check the rest of the huts. George dived over to John's bed. "What happened?"

"The bastard was waiting outside the escape route," John replied. "They must have tumbled to it somehow." He began to curse the redcap with every swear word he could muster. "Christ, George, what am I going to do?" asked John desperately. "Can't you think of something?" But even as he said it, he knew there would be no answer. With the last door bolted on him, he now realised he

41

would have to resign himself to the fact that it was going to be the end of the line to something he had wanted dearly to hold on to.

"Sorry son, I can't help you," George said with a genuine tone of regret in his voice. "It really was important to you, I know." He walked slowly away to his own bed while John lay back staring up at the ceiling trying desperately to blank out the thoughts rushing through his mind. It was no use, it was all over.

4

It was morning again, and he awoke still dressed in his uniform and weary from a restless sleep. The whole episode suddenly came back to him as the partial drug of sleep wore off. Today was to be the day of Judas to him, when he would reluctantly have to bow to the will of the army and throw his own private life out of the window. There was nothing left now but to accept this and make the best of a bad lot. Poor Rita. He tried to kid himself that she would understand, but he knew in his heart it would hurt her as much as it was hurting him. The companies were now assembling for breakfast and he joined their ranks alongside George. "Well, this is our last breakfast in this place," George stated.

Their last breakfast, yes, John thought, but to him it was truly the last supper. His appetite was just not there and he simply picked at the mess in front of him. George, on the other hand, ate ravenously as though he had not had a meal for a week. After eating his own, he quickly gorged John's as well.

"You should eat, Johnnie boy", he said as he shovelled the last morsel into his own mouth, "it's no good going about on an empty gut. Anyway, there's a special parade at ten o'clock. I read about it on the company orders just now. I meant to tell you earlier – we are going to get briefed up on the move we're making."

The move. John's whole existence, he felt, seemed to be hinged on the word 'move'. It was move all the time and then move some more. They never seemed to take root anywhere. It was one big bloody move all the time.

"Where do you reckon, George?" John's voice had a hollow ring about it as he asked. In fact, within himself he did not care much where they went. He knew the only move he would choose was now just a thing of the past and the venture ahead of him was a poor substitute.

"I've heard", said George, "that casino is not going too well and reinforcements went from the camp up the road the other day. Perhaps they have copped their lot and they want some of us silly sods now."

John began to think a little on these statements. He hadn't really given this side of things a lot of thought lately, as life had been one of parades and recreation over the last few weeks, but there now dawned on him the thought that his employers wanted payment for his keep. George's 'copped their lot' came back to him. Funny, he had never seriously thought of dying, charging off into far-flung beaches. Yes, he had done that through his mind a hundred times. Bayonet-charging and emerging victorious had been another of his visions. After all at the pictures, we nearly always win, but now the thoughts took a more

44

serious outlook. He tried to dismiss them from his mind. Anyway it could not happen to him and George. It was impossible. To someone else maybe, yet, but to them, never.

They rose from the table and headed out of the mess-room. From now until ten they would pass their time doing an assortment of fatigues and then the 'big boys' would let them know some bits and pieces of their secret. They would never know the full story, but with the few morsels that would spill off the plate they might be able to piece some picture together although invariably it could be a wrong one.

"Hey, George, do you really think we are winning out here?" The words just simply rolled out of John's mouth.

"How do you mean?" asked George.

"Well, you know, are the high-ups just kidding us along and filling us up with a load of old rubbish just to keep our morale up? I mean, we could be just pushed up the front and get knocked off and who the bloody hell would care about us apart from a cold 'died on active service' in an 'On His Majesty's Service' buff envelope sent to our next of kin?"

"You're morbid, you old sod," George replied. "We won't cop our lot. Don't worry about it; the more you worry, the worse it seems."

This simple philosophy seemed to be the key to George's whole existence. John felt sure that not even an earthquake right under his feet would shake him. John decided not to dwell on the subject. Perhaps George was right.

Before long they were both busily engaged in sweeping out a row of Nissen huts, one of the easier fatigues they had managed to skive onto. As they pitched into their chores, John's mind constantly switched to Rita. A feeling of deep loss and injury to his mind prevailed, and he wondered why with all the wonders of science, no one yet had found a cure for this type of ache, a pain which only the dragging out of time could heal. Then a sergeant's bellow was heard: "All to the assembly hut", and off they trooped to hear what fate awaited them. Once inside the hut all sitting still on the forms, waiting like a bunch of kids at Sunday school, they began to glance around anxiously to establish the identity of the speaker. Usually, the higher the rank the more important the task ahead, and sure enough their own commanding officer – flanked by the duty adjutant and a flock of junior officers – appeared on the stage before them. He began his speech with the aye old 'I'll make this as brief as possible' routine.

"This unit has been chosen." The words almost made John laugh. 'Been chosen', this was the ancient excuse they all offered when they were about to plant some dirty offering in your lap, but the 'been chosen' bit was the medal they flung in to kid you all that you were someone or something special. He went on: "We are going into action to relieve pressure on some of our comrades who, at the moment, are holding out against some rather heavy odds."

Roughly translated, John thought, this meant that they were going to be flung against old Jerry to stop him

46

slaughtering thousands of our lads who were probably at that moment taking a right bashing somewhere up the line.

"I cannot furnish you with too many details as you are all aware that the place of these operations is a military secret." This was the usual old jollop. In other words, you will soon be sent where we send you, and do what we tell you, and may God have mercy on your soul. Oh, the cunning of all these carefully chosen words, thought John. They hide behind and within them a million potholes. They mean crying, horror, death and destruction, silent whimpering of frightened men, and here they were, just words placed in such a way as to seem harmless enough. And what could this vast assembly of men do about it all? Nothing. Absolutely nothing. Because to protest would be treason, and to run from it, cowardice and disgrace to one's inner being. John glanced around him. What went through the minds of these other men who also listened alongside him? Did they see through this sickly veneer they were being offered; did they see this as an offer to future glory; or as it really was - an excuse to let you chance your life for something you never really knew about? Probably half of the married men were thinking of Joan and the kids, of Emmy, of Liz, but not of the cause for which they were fighting. His thoughts turned to George who sat impassively beside him. Poor old George. To him, gone was the girl in his street, gone to the posh office wallah, who, anyway, was probably cute enough to have invented an excuse to remain in civvy street. What did the boy think now? As for his own thoughts, they were mixed. There was no wife and no lust for the Victoria Cross. He had pride as an Englishman, and only that pride at present kept him from screaming out that this was all wrong.

Sugar-coated pill after pill was slowly rolled down the khaki-clad audience's throat until eventually they ran out, and now they were being dismissed, wondering when this offering of the sacrificial lambs was to take place.

It was not long afterwards that the hint came that no one was to leave camp, and John knew the door to happiness between himself and Rita was well and truly shut. She had to be eliminated from his mind altogether and the scar would have to rely upon time to heal. Outside the hut, little gatherings of boys were running over the CO's words and trying to decipher the hidden meanings behind it all. George mouthed his first offering: "Well, my old son, it looks as though the time's arrived for me and you to show them old Jerries what we can do."

John gave him a rather sour look. "Yeah, I suppose so. It looks as though it won't be long by the way we're confined to camp."

He felt that all he could do now was to go forward with the main crowd. As one of the sheep, there was no turning back. From now on he would be on trial with his comrades and with himself. He would either be what the authorities called a man or what they called a coward.

They were now free for a while to skylark around in general and a game of cricket was in progress. Funny how any little patch of ground could be made to look like a bit of England, if only by the use of a bat and a ball. George was now swiping away, not a bit like Len Hutton, and his running between wickets was more like elephant runs, but still he seemed to be enjoying it. John joined in the general melee and he too began to forget his worries for a while.

48

After a session of this no quarter cricket, the majority of the lads went off to their huts to recuperate on their bunks, and for a while, George and John also joined the sleepers. They simply lazed the rest of the afternoon away and George was counting the lira in his pockets in contemplation of skinning a few old Charlies in an evening card session.

The hut door opened suddenly and Sergeant McQueen appeared. "On your feet, everyone," he ordered. "Listen, and listen carefully. You will all be on parade at 18 hundred hours on the dot. Any man not reporting spot on will be on a charge, understood? You will all be in full marching order."

He was gone as quickly as he had appeared. A buzz of voices began among the boys, and there was a sense that this was it. They were off and soon they would share the high-ups' secret. There was no doubt now that they were being sent up the line. In everyone's heart a strange kind of relief must surely have been settling in. After the weeks of tension, a calm was now upon them, the calm before the storm, portrayed in so many books. Everyone began to sort out his kit; first the cumbersome packs were filled with army essentials, which always, to John's amusement, contained a small sewing kit known as a 'housewife'. Where the hell they would have time to sew from now on, he would never know. Nevertheless it came under the solid old word 'equipment'. George was filling his pack with his accustomed lack of finesse, ramming it all in in any shape or form. John, on the other hand, found it better to fold things as neatly as possible. Outside in the square of ground between the huts, lorries were already beginning to assemble in lines, and the roar of dispatch riders going to and fro could be heard. They still had a few hours left yet before they would be on their way, and John felt a strange emotion: a mixture of calm one moment and a rapid excitement the next as his mind raced through thoughts of the events that must surely come very shortly. His main source of comfort lay in George. This was his mate of long-standing and they would go through to any end together. To John, George represented the big brother, the one who could frighten the bully away at school and the one who, when you were a young kid, would take you by the hand and say: "Hold my hand, it's dark."

The time was now upon them. It had crept slowly by, but surely to the appointed hour of departure and now some of the smiling faces of a few hours before had taken on a grimmer look and men gave each other looks that meant they were glad they would not be alone in the following hours. They hurried silently outside and began to form into their respective companies, the sergeants and corporals barking out orders and officers appearing in small groups. The trucks began to pull up to each company and men started clambering into them. Jeeps filled up with the top brass and before long the whole unit was ready to move. John stared about his truck in the semi-darkness of the interior, where Smudge Smith, Tug Wilson, old Mac and the rest of the rogues he came into contact with during his daily routine were sitting. What were they thinking now? Were they scared inside? Did their hard exterior cloak a sinking sick feeling low down in their guts? And George, sitting beside him, how did the big boy feel? John felt that George's chief worry would be for the birds he had left behind him in Naples. His thoughts were halted for a moment as the truck's engine roared to life. They were off. The leading lorries poured out of the gate and their truck took its appointed place in line.

They had been half an hour on the road and hardly a word had been spoken. John knew that each and every man was in a private world of his own, a world that is used only in one's mind for pleasure or pain; a place where one can bring anything one wishes to life or death; somewhere safe from authority of any kind, save only from God above.

"Anyone want a fag?" The voice broke the silence and hands went out and quickly emptied the proffered packet. Tug Wilson spoke up: "What about a song then, you miserable lot of sods?" He broke into a verse of 'Nellie Dean' and a few wavering voices followed suit, but as soon as it was over no new song took its place and silence once again returned.

An hour passed with very little conversation. Even George was unusually silent and John felt the gloom sinking into his very being. The leading trucks began to slow down and then come to a halt. A few of the boys climbed up to see what was going on. "We are in some kind of port," one of them said. "Anyway there's a fleet of craft of some kind up front."

An atmosphere of tense expectation began to creep over them all. George stirred and started to climb out to have a look and John followed him. Sure enough, a fleet of craft looking very much like Yankee Liberty ships were further ahead. These, thought John, were the boats that all those heroes in the pictures rushed out of when the front flaps were lowered, and here he was now probably going in a real one to try and do the same. But would they all reach the shore as the celluloid boys did? Would they rush out to a symphony of clashing cymbals or to a symphony of cascading, death-dealing shrapnel? The boys he was with were no glamorous bunch of screen fame. They were Taffy, Fred, John and Tom – just ordinary boys from a multitude of assorted streets and towns. A bunch of people thrown together to mete out justice to an enemy of the country in which those streets existed. Perhaps their bodies would not be as lucky as those you could view from the safety of the one-and-nine's. At this moment, John loved them all. They were his flesh and blood. Even the mickey-takers among them were dear to him because he was now about to live or die with them, and at a time such as this, any sins against anyone could be forgiven.

Slowly their lorry inched forward again and once more came to a halt further ahead. The boys from the leading truck were now heading towards the first of the craft and slowly began filing on board. A quick glance proved John right: they were Yankee sailors and indeed they were Liberty boats. Soon their turn came and they all went aboard and sat down in rows. Before long their ship began to ease gently out of port and they were on their way to somewhere only the 'big boys' knew.

Rita! She stormed back into John's memory. Although he had tried to dismiss her as merely another girl in his past, what of her tonight? How can one explain a sense of duty to one's country, a Liberty boat creeping into the Mediterranean, and the tossing away of something two people felt deep down for each other? Theirs had been a love between two people of flesh and blood, something that had no connection with this present set-up. There was no feasible explanation why one throws happiness and ecstasy out of the window for fear of the future and an iron Liberty boat. Yes, it was the duty that did it, duty – God curse that word! If it were not for duty he would have run away and enjoyed the rosy future that youth always saw before its eyes. To hell with enemies and countries, kings and queens, but always the word 'duty' loomed up to snatch away all one's plans. A feeling of utter despair had by now enveloped John and he felt that if he did not try to control his feelings they might turn him into a member of the 'bomb-happy' squad he had heard so much about, even before he had even heard a bomb explode. He glanced around at the others in the boat. Most of the boys seemed tense; some looked ahead of them, others merely stared at the floor. How many cowards were in this boat, John thought, and how many potential Victoria Cross men were seated in those rows? They sat facing each other, unaware of the others' courage and yet, oddly enough, all dependent upon each other. He, too, was a cog in the fantastic role of soldier, and yet, what was he? Was he a runner or a potential medal winner? This was something yet to be answered, and even more frightening, he was not sure of his own ultimate answer.

The boat was ploughing through the water but not too far away from the Italian coastline. John had lost track of the time they had been sailing, but they had been going at a steady pace for quite a while. All at once, in the distance, a rumble was clearly heard. A sound like distant thunder. All eyes in the boat glanced instinctively towards the sound. John's heart began to beat wildly and he half rose from his seat. He glanced at George for reassurance and found it only because he was just sitting still. Thank God for this man, whatever else he lacked, he had a steadying influence, John thought. The sound of heavy gunfire was now unmistakable and the boats were distinctly heading towards it. All the answers to his problems lay on some part of this coastline in front of him: the answer to his mental fears and the answer as to his future as a human being. He would either leave this shore as a proven man, as a craven coward or as a corpse. John prayed in his heart that it would be the first mentioned. As a man he would be able to love again and enjoy the fruits of a settled mind. As a coward he would bear a cross of shame within himself and before the eyes of those about him. As a corpse... He blotted this one out as he could find no mental adjustment to suit this image.

The front flaps of the craft dropped with a splash into the sea, and khaki-clad figures hustled onto the shore. John flew out with the mass, body bent in a semi-crouch as if about to crawl on hands and knees. There was confusion at first, hoarse orders being mouthed, and nobody really knew where exactly to go or what to do. George was quickly alongside John. Grim-faced, he just nodded towards a hole caused by a mortar bomb. "In here," he said quickly. They swiftly leaped in, and for a moment recovered their breath. George scrambled up the side of the hole to see what the rest of the boys were doing. He slid back down. "Come on, John, the officers are going forward, let's go." The pair of them scampered out quickly and began to follow a mixture of officers, NCOs and men. A screaming whine and everyone dropped like stones to the ground. Another scream, and another – this John knew was the German mortar commonly known as the Moaning Minnie. The moan was more frightening than the explosion that signalled its disintegration.

Everyone seemed to be like animals, some crawling on hands and knees, some erect, others zigzagging from side to side, but all going the one way – forward. What mental torture must some of them be going through, thought John. His mind was surprisingly alert but he was amazed at his sudden calmness. Crash! Another shell exploded much closer to the little group he had joined. Down they all went, and up and off again. Tracers lit the night sky and all manner of sounds could be heard.

And excitement. A mixture of awe and fear as if in the presence of some Almighty power that held the secret of life and death gripped John, an excitement that he had never felt on the training ground. This was real. These noises were killers and no one came back from the mistake allowed during training. Heavier shells were now coming over and George, his breath coming out fast, said: "The bastards have got our range." A chilling sound was heard in the darkness, a scream like an animal in a trap, unmistakably the scream of a human frame in torment. The scream was followed by a monotonous, steady moan. They hurried on; John felt sick inside and sped forward, away from the lost soul's wailing. Who was it? The old sweat, the joker of the company, the young officer? No one would know until later, but the agonised scream was a scar ripped into John's memory for the rest of his life.

"Down everybody, take cover!". The order came from an officer well-known to them all, and everybody went to earth in a flash. They dived into the nearest hole available, and for a moment John felt safe. He glanced up at his dugout companion. It was not his old pal's face – this man was almost ashen in colour. He did not seem to notice John and was repeating over and over again: "Our Father who art in heaven...", the tears streaming down his face and an agonised pleading look heavenwards. A feeling of terror gripped John. No George, and this man was surely going mad. "Please God, help me, please, please help me," The pleading was now developing into a whine. Was he one of those who had laughed at church parade, who had scoffed at the sky pilot? His hands still clawing skyward, this pitiful fellow crawled over to John's side and amid low sobs beseeched his help. But what help had John to offer? Only a word of comfort, a lying word, a word born out of habit like a person saying sorry for every small misdemeanour one makes. A lie, but in itself just the words "I'll try to help you" were in themselves a straw to a drowning man, John knew, and would be of comfort to a fellow human, and he was glad he could utter this falsity. He put one arm about the quivering shoulders in front of him. "Don't worry old mate, we are all right." He felt his own arm tremble even as he said this. But a further barrage of mortar fire sent the poor wretch scurrying into the furthest corner of the hole, digging at the ground with his bare hands like a mole. John could see that the man was reduced to the lowest state of human degradation, and even though his own fears were heavy upon him, a huge surge of pity swept over him. He knew he could not stay a moment longer and with a last look at the heap of shivering khaki, John scrambled up the side of the hole to see what was happening to those about him.

Where was George, old Mac and the others? They were some way ahead of him now, and he hurried on a little faster for fear that they might think he was backing out at the crucial moment. John quickly caught up with the main body of men and scanned their numbers for his pal George. There he was, right in the middle of the bunch.

Relief waved over John as George scurried to his side. "Where have you been?" he asked, his face a little flushed. "I thought you'd copped one; for Christ's sake keep alongside me."

A shout from an officer – "Dig in" – and out came the entrenching tool from the back of men's belts, and to a man they began scratching at the stony ground beneath themselves. Fear hastened their tiny shovels, and before long every man had carved for himself a small sanctuary from the shell-shattered ground. John lay in his shallow dugout and his mind flashed back to the poor devil he had left behind him a short time previously. What was he doing now, that one-time erect soldier, now reduced to a quivering mass? He offered a silent prayer that authority would show mercy in its judgement of a fellow human in his hour of need. "Johnnie-boy, are you there?" The voice came from George, who had sunk his shaft right beside him.

"Yes, I'm okay George," he replied. It was a great comfort just to hear that familiar voice.

A thunderous barrage had again broken out, and by this time, John's initial calmness was gradually deserting him. The tales of what crept up behind a barrage were having some effect on his mind and he began to have visions of grey-clad figures leaping into his position. For a moment panic seized hold of him and he began to shake. "George," he half-shouted in desperation.

"What's up, old son?" The voice floated over, giving the effect of a tranquilising drug.

"Nothing, it's all right," John answered. He began to calm down and mopped his forehead with his begrimed sleeve. He was all right now; his mind was slowly clearing and he once more silently thanked his Maker for creating the big fellow who was at that moment his only link with sanity in this desolate place. It was funny, he thought, how in a situation such as this one's mind played tricks. One minute there was an absolute feeling of depression to be followed next by a quiet calm and the possession of sheer animal alertness.

A head appeared over the top of their dugout and John swiftly brought the barrel of his rifle in line with it. "Hold it." A sigh of relief as he recognised Sergeant McQueen. "We'll be here some time, son", he said in a quiet voice, "so make yourself as comfortable as possible and keep your eyes and ears open. The rations will be brought to you later. So long for now."

He felt a lot better as he sensed some form of organisation getting under way, and this gave John a feeling of security. Also, the heavy barrage had begun to subside a little and apart from sporadic small-arms fire that seemed to be in the distance, it was relatively calm compared with the earlier half-hour.

And now what was to happen? Here he was, thrown onto some strange beach and just sitting in a hole he had frantically scratched out a short time ago, with not the vaguest idea how this almost comic opera situation would turn out. This was not quite the landing he had envisioned in his rehearsals of months ago. Still, here he was, and the brass hats would no doubt find some task for him very shortly. The air was getting chilly so he pulled his coat closer around him. He had lost track of time and anyway, what did time mean for him now? There was no set timetable here. Everything, no doubt, would come in an unpredictable blanket. Did a merciful Creator lie watching man's follies, forever mourning for His earthly creations, for those pieces of clay He had fashioned, and who were now engaged in some mad game of trying to smash each other to pieces? And did He tonight look down on him, John, as an individual? Deep down John felt as though there must be an overall power somewhere, and in the darkness, there and then, he placed his hands together and with a faltering whisper began as he used to in his Sunday- school days: "The Lord is my shepherd, I shall not want..." As the last of his whispers completed the end of the 23rd Psalm, John felt a burden lift from him and a renewed faith in himself settle upon him. He also knew in his heart that it was only because he was on his own in this small patch of earth that he was not embarrassed to pray. Had the others been watching, he would not have had the guts; nevertheless he felt sure his Maker would overlook this small point.

A shower of small stones fell into John's trench again and he clutched hard onto his rifle and stared upwards. It was dear old George looking down. "Hello son, you all right?"

"Sure", the elation at seeing his mate made him sound genuinely happy. "Any idea what's going on?"

"I ain't got a clue." For once George was stumped. "The only thing I can think of is we're waiting for daybreak and then we might try to push on again. Anyway, how's this bloody hole of yours? Mine's about two foot short and it's proper crampy."

"This one's exactly the opposite of the Savoy, but its somewhere to hide."

George suddenly stopped and then whispered "someone's coming!" and slithered off back to his own dugout. Another hand soon appeared and to John's relief it turned out to be the rations corporal. He quickly rolled a few tins to John and was gone on his rounds. John's jack-knife flashed round the rim of a tin of beans and before long it was empty. He took a swig from his water bottle and had a look at the other tins for a tasty dessert. There it was, a tinned sultana pudding. What sheer luxury he thought, certainly in this place, it seemed like manna from heaven. John lay back after his mixed grill and apart from the ever constant knowledge of where he was, could quite easily have gone off to sleep. The artillery barrage had died off altogether and it was easy to lapse into a false sense of security. Whatever else he did, he must certainly not think that the danger was over. Funny though, he mused, they had been mortared and shelled by someone he could not see and yet those people could bring sudden death to him and his mates without ever having known them. What a crazy set-up the world had got itself into! He wondered what the fellows on the other side thought of all this. Were those tales of fanatical storm troopers real or something cooked up to keep one on one's toes? He had read in books of the fearsome deeds that some of the Jerries had done in the '14–18 battles, but did this new generation still hold this lust for war and inherit the savagery of their parents? Or were they at this moment crouched, as he was, in a hole somewhere not far from him? John was more inclined to think that that was the way things were; after all, human nature endowed all people with the same number of faculties even though they speak different languages. Nevertheless he knew they were trained, as indeed he had been, to kill all those who fought for the opposite side, and the survivor who would triumph in the end would be the more coordinated state-machine. It was not a trial of strength of soldiers' arms and legs, or any bodily attributes, but where the soldiers as a whole were placed at the critical point in time. At this particular point in time, John felt he knew nothing. He left this entirely to those out of his reach, and strangely enough, he had an explicit faith in their abilities to carry him and his mates through, even though he knew it was his life and theirs that was being held in their decisions. Perhaps today or tomorrow, one ill-timed order could send him and many more like him into a situation where they could lose their lives needlessly. John shuddered at the thought and thanked God he did not bear such a responsibility. It was not all fun and games at the top, and perhaps they had a heavier cross to bear than he, John imagined.

An uncanny silence hung over this shattered area now, and John began to feel a sense of acute anxiety as to what was being cooked up by the opposing element. Were they slithering silently forward on their bellies as he had learned to do on the training fields back home, or were they waiting for their leader to utter some animal-like cry and come charging over in hordes? Either prospect was no comfort to him and he stealthily moved himself to raise his eyes over the side of the hole. Much to his relief there were no shadowy shapes, no messengers of doom, just a shell-broken acre of earth stretched in front of him. Suddenly from apparently nowhere, a head popped out of the ground a few feet away. It was George.

"Wotcher my old son, it's bloody quiet around here ain't it?" he whispered.

"You're not kidding," said John. "It's too quiet. They know we're here, so why suddenly leave us alone like this after the lashing they dished out when we landed?"

"I don't know", mumbled George, "it's bleeding funny to me as well."

A sudden whine in the distance alerted both men. It was getting increasingly louder. "Lay down quick". George ordered sharply, and his head disappeared from John's view. The whine became a nerve-racking sound as the Stuka dive-bombers appeared from nowhere. They began their suicidal dive towards earth only to pull sharply skyward after unloading their parcels of death. Wave after wave began to pour down, one after the other, and John found himself flat on his face gripping a handful of tiny stones in each fist until the whites of his knuckles showed. He glanced fearfully upwards to watch the ballet of death-dealing machines diving one after the other. They seemed to be directly above him and in his imagination it was as though they were concentrating solely on his dugout. He was still unhurt physically, but mentally it was the biggest hiding he had ever taken. His body racked with an uncontrollable fear, his stomach became knotted, his mouth trembled, and his tongue was not moist enough to lick his lips. He felt a strong desire to run and run from this place and never to stop until this dreadful noise ceased, and yet some quiet voice inside his head was whispering 'this is part of your test'. He implored this insane reasoning to leave him, but it was not to be vanquished, and John knew it would be there for the rest of his life to mock him if he did the intelligent thing and run away.

The whine was dying as quickly as it had begun and once more the earth fell silent as though after a heavy downpour of rain. A shout not far from his dug- out sickened him for a moment. "Stretcher-bearers, over here!" Once more he looked over the top, comforted by the sound of familiar voices and yet chilled by the need of their calling. Some poor bastard had copped it! The stones dug into John's knees as he crawled in panic towards George's slit, but the big fellow's head appeared before he reached it. John almost collapsed with relief and without a word to George he scurried back to his own rat hole. He lay there flat on his back, worn out, as though he had run a thousand miles. His breath was laboured and his mind was in turmoil. John suddenly felt like an old man, a longing to go home and lie down between crisp, white sheets and to sleep and sleep and not to wake for years, and when he did eventually wake, to go out into a place of beauty to smell flowers and to laugh and to have peace of mind to have the everyday pleasures that found no place in this hell on earth, to love like the youngster that he was, to hold Rita and to tell her a thousand times that he loved her. But Rita was gone. Everything beautiful and kind had disappeared from here, nothing but fear and destruction was left and you could only court either one of these deadly maidens. No flowers bloomed here to exude their pleasant fragrances; there was only the perfume of death. The acrid smell of cordite was a poor substitute for the simple smell of a daisy in an English field. Please God, put back the flowers, turn the brown grass green again, let the stretcher-bearers have no need for their tasks, let man shake hands with man, let love reign supreme in the hearts of one and all, leave the youngsters their heritage, let them have their time to love their Ritas, let them have time to see their sons and daughters grow into peace-loving citizens, and above all, cease this dreadful carnage. This prayer has been in man's mind since time immemorial, a phantom kingdom born from despair, a place built only in the mind, a fantasy that could but never would take place. It was an opiate to John, a built-in mechanism of the brain, the safety valve that flooded the mind in torment and saved the body it served.

John's mind returned to reality, and the wonderful kingdom of his imagination faded from sight. Nothing but a cold dugout was now before him and an area of potential danger.

In himself, John knew that the events of the past hour had been a severe test of his courage. He had not run, but his whole system and mind had screamed out to him to do the sane thing and run. He began to wonder what had kept him there. The answer lay deep down from whence the small voice had come. It was a form of cowardice, a cowardice that stems from not wanting to be different from the pack. If he had run away, he knew he would have been branded a deserter, and yet to run and be branded thus, and knowing this, would have required courage of a different kind. His had been the courage of the main pack, and this was the courage that was recognised and even gained medals. To try the other brand brought ignominy and punishment. He shut out the small voice of conscience and began to applaud silently his own choice, but always in the background, a mocking laugh oozed its way through, taunting, annoying, scrambling through every argument he put in its path, and finally cutting out with a 'but to oneself be true'. He knew it could never really be banished and John would have to live with it. He also knew he would betray it a thousand times more yet.

"On your feet everybody!" The order came loud and clear and the sound of small stones rolling back into holes brought John swiftly back to earth. He sprang quickly out of his slit trench and was amazed to see how close some of the others had been to him. There was Mac and good old 'Tug and the camp joker Smudge, and numerous others. The ones he knew as friends all seemed to be still there, and of course good old George was quickly by his side. "What do you think of those screaming bastards? They frightened the bloody life out of me!"

John nodded assent:, "Me too", he stated simply, not giving a clue as to the nightmare of torment they had brought to him.

They were now trudging forward at a steady pace, the screaming demons that had sprayed death on them must have returned to their nests. They came to a small hill and the leading officer ordered the men to ground. He, together with a sergeant, crawled their way to the top and looked over to see what lay below. After a while, the sergeant returned and signalled his men to follow him. They reached the top and looked down into the minute valley where a few dozen white-painted houses nestled. To them everything appeared quiet, but knowing the cunning of an enemy this could be a trap. The night was coming to an end and dawn was creeping its way over the horizon, the air was not yet warm, but John knew that before long the sun would at least add some sparkle to life.

Sergeant McQueen and Corporal Grant were now in some kind of earnest conversation with Captain Logie, and from hand gesticulations it seemed that these two NCOs were being sent down the slope to really find out what lay in the village below them. This turned out to be the case, as a few minutes later they began to edge their way down towards the valley below. Captain Logie lay down with his field glasses poised to follow the descent of his officers and the rest of the men lay there clutching at the various motley of weapons shared out among them. John held his rifle close to his side. This he had been taught was his best friend at times such as these, but this friend gave but one greeting – there was no cheery hello from this friend, he gave only the devil's handshake and spewed but the greeting of death, and yet with this piece of metal and wood he had fused an unreal comradeship. George, on the other side of John, had an automatic Sten gun of which he had always been proud. He had often teased John about the numbers he could knock over before John could put another round into the breech of his Lee-Enfield. But how did one count glory? Surely not in the number of dead bodies at one's feet.

A sharp splutter of automatic fire from down the slope somewhere ahead of them brought an alertness to each man lying at the top. Captain Logie stiffened and gazed more intently downwards. Moments later the form of Sergeant McQueen reappeared over the brow of the hill and from his face it was apparent that Corporal Grant would not be coming back.

More conversation between officer and sergeant, and John could now almost read the hand movements like a deaf man lip-reads. The hand signals during their conversation this time meant only one thing: Corporal Grant had been killed while on active service and the appropriate buff envelope would duly be delivered to some pleasant council house in Edinburgh or to some slum in the Gorbals, but the message to the inhabitants would read the same the world over. It would simply mean that a fit, virile young life had ended in its prime, and the wife, children or parents, or whomever the survivors were to him, would just have to accept that the gay laugh, the brooding moods, the smile as a small child, or any endearing traits that this man had ever possessed were not to be repeated again, and would never again be heard, except in their memories. It was truly ashes to ashes and dust to dust. For John there would be sadness for some time at the loss of a comrade, but for one of those other poor souls, perhaps a lifetime of mourning lay ahead.

Captain Logie had left the sergeant keeping watch down below, and was motioning the men to come closer to him. In half-whispers he began to explain that the village was still occupied and that Corporal Grant had met his death by disturbing a German sentry. Any more explanation was smartly cut off as mortar shells began to rain down on their hilltop. "Disperse!" His hoarse tone added urgency to the already scrambling boots. Men ran in every conceivable direction but cover was sadly lacking, and in desperation some men tried to drag the sparse tufts of grass over their exposed bodies. Some were in full flight down the hill, knowing at least that at the bottom there were a few dugouts. John soon joined this group with George galloping alongside him. It was evident that the sentry who had dealt with Grant was now the instigator of this bombardment. He had obviously warned his trench men of the threat that had lain at the top of the valley, but if he only knew how quickly that threat was now dispersing he would no doubt be feeling a lot easier. The confusion at the top of the hill was gradually sorting itself out and everybody was rushing headlong to where John's group had fled, save for some forms that still remained motionless and would never go anywhere again, except back to the earth. Huddled together in two's in the deeper dugouts at the bottom of the hill, they awaited orders for their next move in the chess game, one and all aware that the wrong order could mean check-mate. John cast his eyes toward the officer in whom they had placed their trust and hopes; his young face wore the worried look of a much older man. At the same time he had the aura of the university graduate about him – the type who wore a bowler in civvy street, lives in a neat suburban house, goes to the office at 09.00 and returns home promptly at 17.30. Certainly he was the type of whom one felt a little confused as to whether to address him as 'mate' or 'sir'.

John did not envy his task, for now all the posh veneer of the gentleman would be of no assistance; it was strictly military stuff now.

The officer scanned the line of serious faces around him, presently halting on the nearest pair of stripes. "Corporal Hogarth, I want you to take 12 men and try to outflank the enemy in the village below. You will approach it from the left; another NCO will lead a further party in the same manoeuvre from the right. Each NCO will take a Very pistol and the first one in position will signal in this manner. Try to remember that as soon as the first light is sent up, the enemy will have a rough idea of your positions and your aim, so speed is essential from both parties. On arrival of both parties to their positions and both lights answered, the two parties will then begin to close in on the valley and the remainder of us will attempt to come in from the hilltop above. Is that clear to you all?" Corporal Hogarth and Corporal Kane both nodded. "Then select your men."

John crept closer to George. If he was chosen they must both go. They were duly selected by Corporal Kane and after a brief check of grenades and ammo they were stealthily on their way. As they moved forward, John thought of the cold clinical manner they were termed as parties – not as humans, but parties – and the age-old outflanking trick that was now being attempted was always fine for a few laughs in their training sessions back home. Even an umpire on their manoeuvres had once declared both outflanking parties had killed each other off. Then it was one hilarious joke, but now they were playing for keeps and mistakes could not be rectified by the umpire's decision. There was only one umpire here, and to be on the wrong side of him meant being six foot under, wrapped in an old army blanket and with a small wooden cross to mark the spot. John shuddered at the thought and whispered to George: "How long do you reckon it would take us to get them in line?"

"About an hour", George replied, "unless in the meantime they go up the bloody hill and wipe that lot out waiting up there."

John had not even given this a thought, but in George's blunt summing up of the military situation there was a distinct possibility of that happening, after all they did know they were up there and now that their ranks were much thinner; if this happened and the Jerries took the hilltop while they took the valley, they would be back to square one.

I bet that not even the boardroom brigade had even thought this situation through. But with them, a few moves with the salt shaker overpowering the vinegar bottle, and eventually capturing the pepper pot, the situation would have sorted itself out, thought John. They kept as close to hedges as possible, weaving their way across field after field, some ploughed and making their hoots feel heavier with the clogging soil. Always with this outflanking activity one took a long time to get to the target area, but it usually paid dividends. "Down everybody!" Corporal Kane's voice had an urgent ring. They were flat on the ground to a man. Before them, a belt of trees obscured their view but it was obvious that the target area lay beyond the trees. They all crept closer together and before long Kane appeared in the midst of them. He gave them a quick briefing: "This is it", he said, "beyond those trees is a long wall about 200 feet away. We'll all make for it when I fire the Very pistol. The other team, we hope, will be doing roughly the same thing if they've arrived. Take up positions for firing beyond that wall. If we're not spotted on our way to the wall, all the better. Is that clear to everyone?" They all nodded, and John pressed his rifle closer to his side.

George gave a grim smile. "Keep by me, old son; it'll be okay, you'll see."

The Corporal's hand was poised and away went the little ball of light from his pistol. "Now everyone, run for your lives." Their bodies were geared into action and away they all sped, crouched, heads down, some falling onto their knees only to rise seconds after and scramble towards the wall ahead that seemed miles away. In a heap they all arrived and lay breathless for a moment. Had their luck held? There was no doubt that the Germans had seen the light go up, but did they know how close to them the attackers were? A sigh of relief; there, in the sky, was the brother Very light from the party on the other side and no fire had been directed on them – yet. Perhaps they had made the wall without being spotted. The Corporal glanced around to make sure everybody was with him. "Right boys, our next move is our final one and providing you all keep your heads, we sleep in houses tonight. Good luck everyone! Let's go."

He was over the wall and without exception every man was on his heels. There in front of them lay the village. Suddenly all silence was shattered by the rapid fire of a Spandau automatic. Intermingled with this tune of death were the horrific childlike screams of the charging men, and John's throat, though parched with fear, also gave a spontaneous yell. A handful of grey uniforms loomed up, but these men had their hands above their heads and John and George swept past them onto the nearest house. Quickly opening the door, a grenade was flung inside and the door once more shut fast. The roar of the explosion sounded and a quick search was made for any survivors. There were none. All that remained was the shattered body of a soldier of the Reich clutching a broken Spandau machine gun. For a moment John gazed in morbid fascination at the dead man, he felt a deep sense of guilt because he had been instrumental in this man's end. His hands were trembling – the same hands that could have warmly clasped this dead man's hands in a verbal agreement had settled any issue between them with a pineapple-shaped lump of metal. There was no physical victory, no moral one either, all that had been settled in cold fact was that one man had taken another's life because he had held the advantage at the critical moment. There was a sadness in it all, but it was an absolute necessity if one was to survive. To John, death was becoming part of his very existence. He found himself waiting for the next batch of bodies to be found. They had a curious effect upon him. For those who had died in obvious agony he found himself near to tears, and yet for those with a look of serenity on their faces, he seemed to gain a great peace of mind.

Resistance had collapsed and a small ragged band of German prisoners were filtering past under the stern gaze of one of Kane's men. As John strode out into the small village street he could see men of his own party mingling with men of Hogarth's. The simple operation had been a complete success. Soon Captain Logie was again among them, having descended from the hill, and was giving out orders right, left and centre.

George loped easily alongside John. "You okay? That's a few less of the bastards, but Smudgie copped it!" Smudgie! The very word froze John in his tracks. Poor old Smudgie, always good for a laugh and that couple of bob was always there till payday. "Right through the nut," George said. "Don't suppose he knew what hit him. Still, it could've been any one of us." He continued: "Come on Johnnie boy, cheer up! We sleep in houses tonight."

To sleep in houses – this simple luxury the man in civvy street took for granted. To sleep in houses tonight, and part payment of the mortgage was the khaki-clad brother soldier by the name of Smudgie. The sentries were posted and men were allotted their houses. Inside, wondrous tales of that long-forgotten place – home – were being spun. George lay stretched out on the floor, his eyes riveted to the ceiling.

"You know", he started, "my mum had a lamp like that when I was a kid, and I hated the sight of it because she would always turn it off in my bedroom when I'd been larking about. It was beautiful while it was on, but it was out most of the time."

"You should have bloody well behaved yourself a bit more then", chided Tug Wilson, "then you could've watched it all night."

A trickle of laughter went round the room like a silver ripple. It was not the laughter that stems from a very funny story, but the sound of men's throats that are in a place of sanctuary for a brief space of time; the laugh of a man who, recovering consciousness, finds he is still alive and is glad to he living.

George did not bat an eyelid; he just carried on staring at this thing of glory. John gazed about him. Kane was sitting in the corner just puffing away at his fag; only an hour earlier he must have felt like a field-marshal leading his men. He had done just that, and no man could fault his courage. And Ron, the stern-faced farmer, John could never remember his other name, but what did it matter? He was reclining, arms folded, perhaps thinking of cows, pigs or sheep. And what of little Taffy with the slight squint in his left eye; was it the Eisteddfod or Blodwen back home? All these men were somewhere in thought, and it was John's guess that home was not far away. Time passed in an absolute orgy of sheer nonsense for a while. Every single item that was vaguely funny was trundled out, even the story of the seductive blonde whom Tug Wilson admitted lived next door to him and who had fallen for his wiles after a period of wooing was told. This had been a close secret with Tug for years as some of the boys lived not far from him, but now his inhibitions seemed to have vanished and skeletons from his cupboard were coming out thick and fast. Farmer Ron admitted to a little rustling down at his country farm. The atmosphere in that small room was England, and John found pleasure in the fact that he too was one of them. A silence fell as George, in conversation, inadvertently mentioned Smudgie's name. There was always a sort of reverence at the mention of a dead man's name, but there was also forgiveness for the living at the mistakes in speech that mortal man can make.

Some of the boys in a house up the road had filled an old tin bath with fat; a whole dismembered pig had found its resting place in the boiling oil, and an emissary from them had arrived with an invitation to join the feast. There was no need to ask a second time. There was a rush of army boots and within a few minutes the luncheon was in progress. No dinner-jacketed affair this one – it was 'dress optional'. The smell of roasting pork wafting down the street had hastened their progress, and on arrival they saw that one or two of the gentlemen of little etiquette had already gorged themselves into oblivion. Intermingled with the pork bubbling away in the bath, enough potatoes were being boiled to feed a brigade. John had never enjoyed a meal more. He stabbed into the bath and brought out on the end of his bayonet a piece of pork huge enough for the Sunday joint back home and as many potatoes as he could eat. What a treat to have fresh cooked food instead of the old tinned rations! Again they started to chat and also learned with regret that two of the boys were lost from the Hogarth party, but to his own shame, John found himself now beginning to dismiss rather more lightly the loss of anyone but personal friends. The meal they were all enjoying had by now developed into a sort of Roman orgy, minus the dancing girls, but one of the boys cavorting about the room like Salome was putting on a great show. Notwithstanding the fact that there were no girls and no beer, this was the next best thing – a good bellyful of food.

The door opened and in walked Captain Logie. He smiled, glancing round at Salome who had finished his dance pretty abruptly. "Carry on lad", Logie laughed, "you look quite entrancing." A roar of laughter greeted this remark and the poor fellow coloured a deep red. "That looks nice. I suppose you don't mind my diving in. After all, even officers eat now and again." A dozen or so bayonets prodded the mass in the bath at once, eager to give of what they had had. They had grown to respect this man. He was what they were beginning to term 'one of the boys'. Their superior in rank he may have been, but to them at that moment he was just another hungry soldier. He sat himself down among them and began to eat, and this small gesture ended any doubts some may have had that he was stuck-up or snobbish. Some of the men were dozing off, and John could see George's head slowly dropping onto his chest. He, too, felt a tiredness, but this time it was a more comfortable sort of weariness. But they could not remain in this one house all night, which was by now drawing in. They would have to disperse eventually to their respective positions and plainly the Captain was informing the NCO of this. Soon John found himself once more on the move, together with the rest of the full-bellied group. George shuffled up alongside. "What a gutful!" He belched. "Fit for a king that lot was." John smiled at George's description, 'a gutful.' None of the niceties for that big fellow.

The NCOs had detailed men for the takeover of the sentries and John knew he was due on the midnight till 02.00 watch. George, the lucky devil, had got out of it altogether, but still, he was never found wanting if he had been chosen. All men in the meantime were to clean their weapons and assist in general with arrangements being made for securing their position. How long they were to stay was just a matter of assumption among the fellows, but on a general consensus of opinion it would not be for long. At least they knew that for the next few hours, barring unforeseen events, they were to remain in this valley of rest. They reached their allotted house and began rifling cupboards for anything of value and anything that could be slept upon. Some men wandered from room to room just mooching about, a few curses here and there as large army boots came into contact with recumbent bodies attempting to get some sleep. George had secured a position for the two of them in the corner of the room. A wise old bird this fellow, he always did preach that if you sat in a corner, no one could creep up behind you. He had also collared the only available mattress and was successfully warding off a succession of thieving hands that were tugging at it.

"Hurry up, John," he shouted. "Lie down here and stamp on a few of these shifty geezers' hands." Eventually their place was secured, the enemy destroyed and they sank back triumphantly into the finest bed in the room. It seemed to be only a few minutes that he had lain down when a faint nudging had John sitting bolt upright. "Come on son, you're on guard." He clambered slowly into his greatcoat, and rubbing sleep from his eyes, John walked out into the night air. It was cold after the warmth of the room and he fastened his coat up to the neck. Kane was escorting him to relieve the sentry, and before long they reached the vantage point where he was stationed. He was glad to see them and John knew the comforting feeling the other man now felt as his turn was finished. A brief nod and Kane and the relieved sentry were gone again, and John began his two-hour stint. The old routine back home was either to start counting the number of paces it took from point A to point B, or to count the number of any objects nearby that were countable. In this manner, one's duration of duty seemed to fly by. But that was back home. Here one had to be alert. The old 'halt, who goes there?' routine was deadly serious and no mistakes could be rectified after the trigger finger had been squeezed. John peered into the gloom. What was that shape over there? Nothing... or was it a man? No, it was not moving, but then that's what he had been taught to do – to stalk up on men. John gave the object another searching glance and convinced himself that it was nothing. All the same, he found his eyes constantly returning to the same spot. Other objects were now assuming sinister outlines and he felt surrounded by hordes of gremlins intent upon doing his mind harm, but he steeled himself to the fact that his mind was playing tricks. The solid piece of wood and metal he clutched at his side would soon come to his aid if the need arose. Old George would be well away now, John thought, safe and snoring away on the old mattress and here he was keeping

77

watch so that George could snore in safety. The lucky bastard.

How quiet the night appeared now, and yet only a few hours ago man had killed man just for a few acres of land. If God looked down on this scene, surely He could see the error of it all, for one could picture beauty if one looked hard enough. At the same time, one's own imagination could bring pictures of terror purely through thought. Would this senseless slaughter go on for ever? There must be an end, and then for how long would there be peace? For a few years and then would it begin all over again? All these things raced through John's mind as he stared out into the darkness, a darkness that covered him from preying eyes and yet a darkness that gave him no advantage either. A rustle to the right froze him rigid for a moment: John's rifle flew upwards as a paper wrapper flew past him disturbed by a sudden faint breeze. John's facial muscles loosened again as the piece of paper continued on its course. Such a little thing, but with nerves stretched like piano wire it gave the whole system quite a turn.

An hour passed, just one to go. How many more times within the next hour would his body's alarm system be geared into action? John felt tired now, but he must not relax. More than his own life depended on his alertness; the lives of his pals were also in his keeping. He began to think back on the events that had brought him here: the boat from England, the interminable training, Rita. He paused in thought. Rita was gone, and yet those tender hours could still be recalled – the mind was a wonderful storehouse. John felt a pang of sorrow and regret and wished time could be turned back for just a while to say the unsaid things; but time was like the sea – it came in and it was gone – only in memory could one have it back, and John was lucky he could still remember. There were other poor devils whose every faculty now lay dormant under Italian soil. One, two, three, he began to count to himself, always when he reached 60 he knew one more minute of his watch was over, but strangely he never seemed to go on counting. It seemed so long to count for just one minute. John pondered what the German sentries were thinking of as they patrolled about: did they have similar little tricks that helped to pass the time? Apart from the rustling piece of paper, John's watch that night had been uneventful, for which he was grateful. Half-an-hour to go and then he would sink back into that glorious old mattress. But, hold it! There was an unmistakable sound of someone treading softly towards him. John lay silently down on the ground, rifle pointing in the direction of the footsteps. "Halt, who goes there?" His voice sounded hoarse. "Friend!" The unmistakable voice of Captain Logie rang out. "Advance friend and be recognised." The old malarkey, but this time in deadly earnest.

Logie came alongside John. "Just checking up," he said. "Everything in order?"

"Yes sir," John replied feeling a little ashamed at his rather panicky challenge.

"Good," mumbled Logie. "Good night." And he was gone.

"Goodnight", muttered John, "what's left of it." Good job he had been on his toes; there's nothing worse than being found wanting on sentry go. Just a quarter left. John felt that he would willingly give a whole week's pay for a good cup of tea, but that lot snoring away back there certainly would not have the kettle on for his homecoming. Still, this wasn't Rita he was going back to, and he might still manage to make a cup of sludge that rejoiced under the name of cocoa. Once more the distinct sound of footsteps, this time more than one pair. No doubt his relief, but no chances must be taken, and the old challenge was again repeated and answered satisfactorily. A brief exchange of greetings and John was off, back to his haven of rest. It was once more Corporal Kane escorting him back. "Everything okay out there?" he queried.

"Hell yes", John replied, "everything's fine."

They went back to John's quarters and Kane left him to amble off towards his own billet while John crept as silently as possible through the front door. The sound of nasal whistling greeted him as he passed one door and John knew they were far away from war at that moment. He tiptoed into his own room. There lay the big fellow, slantwise across the mattress, snoring his head off. John bent over him, picked up his legs and placed him straight, not a move from George. By Christ, thought John, good job he was not one of the Jerries. They would have all been prisoners-of-war by now. Still, that's why he had been on sentry duty: to see that precisely that did not happen. John looked around for signs of any tea or cocoa and found none, so he contented himself with a swig from his water bottle – the wretched stuff was warm and sickly, but it quenched his thirst at least. Off came his coat, off came his boots, and John sank down to rest, giving the big boy a bit of a shove over to make room for himself.

5

All too soon his hours of rest ended, and as always, John felt dead-tired on waking, but that was all part of living and it was one of the worst parts. Most of the boys were on their feet putting on the odd garments they had discarded, and were no doubt wondering what this day had in store for them. George was still lying down like a cast off rag doll. "Come on, get up." John said giving George a bit of a thump: "There will be hell to play if McQueen catches you; the Corporal's called us twice already."

George began to stir. "Sod the lot of them", he muttered fiercely, "I'll be bloody glad when this caper's over."

He had hardly finished his irate tirade when McQueen walked in, followed by both Corporals Hogarth and Kane.

"Parade outside in ten minutes," he commanded. Turning to both corporals, he instructed them to see that the men were in possession of all the equipment they had brought with them. McQueen then marched off smartly as though he were on the drill square back home.

"It gets on your nerves all this load of old codswallop," George continued, "you never settle down for more than a day and they drag you off again." Poor old George! He had got the miseries today, John thought; still, everyone gets that disease at some time or the other, and he was no exception. "Wonder what's going on today", George went on; "I suppose half the bloody Jerry army will be after us."

They began to assemble outside. It was very chilly at that hour of 06.00, and no one felt exactly at his best. Logie appeared as neat and spruce as always, quick conversations with the NCOs, and they were then ordered into aircraft formations, marched off out of the village that had given them shelter and a great deal of comfort for the night. George was still cursing and complaining about the rotten old army and John could not help but smile. He had often felt the animosity himself but was now rather resigned to the fact that they had a job to do and that was that. As John glanced at the boys marching along beside him he also remembered that some who were there yesterday were not with them now, and their moans and groans about their present situation were trivial compared with the price the boys had paid the previous day. John thought back to the village they had just vacated. It was funny, but all the civilians had left it on their entry, and John began to wonder what had happened to these people. Had they felt that they must run from the intruder into their private lives, or were they just plain scared out of their wits? It must be heart rending, John thought, to just abandon one's life possessions, everything one had worked hard to save for, and leave it all behind, knowing that strangers' hands would no doubt forage through things that had been precious to them. But this was part of the price of war and humans had learned to suffer the indignities thrust upon them through war. John felt an anger rise inside him. What if it had happened in England?

They were marching at a steady pace and beginning to warm up a little, the white dust covering their khaki giving it two-toned colours. The white dust was a feature of this part of the country; it got into everything and parched one's throat into the bargain. John looked forward to the time when he would be striding up a street in dear old Blighty, a packet of civilian wages in his pocket and no fear of any blast that could send him to eternity at any minute. Yes, that would come one day soon and he could have such a beer-up with some of these boys that they would probably take a week to recover from it. An aircraft screamed overhead, but it was a friendly one, and anxious eyes of some of them gazed steadfastly in front of them to whatever lay ahead, to victory or defeat, only the Gods knew, along this winding road disturbed now and again by the odd horse and cart with the impassive Italian farmer aboard. A shout was heard from up front: "Take a rest." Everybody relaxed at the side of the road, some flat out, others holding their feet as if administering some magic balm through the thick leather. George flopped down. "About bloody time too", he uttered moodily, "my dogs are killing me!"

"Never mind", sympathised John, "nobody's whacked us one yet and it's a day nearer the end of it".

"There's no sodding end," George muttered. "There's no bloody end. It'll end when they've made us all into corpses."

"Christ George, what's the matter with you today? You're a proper miserable bastard."

"Can't help it, it's just one of those things, everything's black." His words were drowned by a scream of a mortar bomb, which landed just short of the road itself. Splinters of steel whistled through a bush that had been to the right of them.

"Everybody take cover!" The order was unnecessary as the majority of the boys had already done so. John was in the ditch at the side of the road as the second bomb came over. This one hit the middle of the road and the noise was far greater than the first. He huddled down in the ditch awaiting the third. He did not have long to wait. It came with a deafening roar and this time claimed some victims, the chilling cry of a man in pain could clearly be heard, not one for now several had joined the eerie wail and the nerves of John's body signalled panic. But no, resist them, they were not to be obeyed. Destroy your natural feelings, kick them out: you are a machine, a product of the training ground. The finished product should be able to cope with any situation, or so the establishment said in the books. John scurried down the ditch towards the moans of his comrades, no heroic dragging a man out of no-man's-land under heavy fire, just a wave of sympathy towards the cries of pain that were filling his ears. McQueen, his mouth half open, his eyes in a fixed stare upwards, both hands tightly gripped around his stomach, gone from this world with no goodbyes, no handshake to signal his exit, just a lump of dead human flesh. 'One sergeant army for the use of', as the quotation goes. John stumbled past him in horror, another inert form, face down, the white dust on his uniform now patched with red. His mind began to boggle at the majesty of death, so all-consuming, so swift, so ultimate; it scythed down the good and the bad with the same bloody axe, there was no discrimination. But its final taunt was yet to come, for the figure John now stood over, ashen faced and near its maker, was George. His dear friend, confidant, helper, all that was comradeship embodied in khaki, now lay at his feet whimpering, blood spattered, trembling, and not dying at all as the cinema portrayed. No, this broken friend was taking the painful road to heaven or hell. He was twitching and gurgling and making spasmodic movements to rise to his feet, as a slaughtered animal at the abattoir. John recoiled in abject horror at the form he had come to know in life. He wanted to hold this man to him now more than at any other time, and yet his hands were frozen with revulsion; his tongue was too, and he felt a lump in his throat, a sinking choking feeling. He fought back tears; George was on his way out, he had 'copped his lot' (in his own words) and yet surely this could not be for real, not this way. Pals and muckers don't go this way. It must be a dream. This heap at his feet was not going out like this, they would make him well again. Foolish fancy, idle dream, a rationalisation that no amount of wishful thinking would ever save the big fellow. He was down at George's side now, whispering those words everyone whispers when he holds a man in pain. For one thing he was grateful: that he had at last got over his own fear of this dying friend, and this time just for once, it would he his hand that would try to guide George through his darkness.

"George", he whispered, "you hurt bad?" His friend's eyes gazed unseeing past John's shoulders, his body shuddering and twitching, blood oozing from his uniform. John knew his question would never be answered and that it was a foolish one to ask. He had always imagined death as a dignified affair, but now how dignified could one look with a body racked with pain, with flesh torn, lying in a ditch. No, poor George was a loser again. He had lost his girl to the posh officer wallah and now he was losing again. He was losing in the way he would have wanted to die; he had always said when he snuffed it that he wanted it to be in bed one wintry night. All his past little funny sayings flooded through John's consciousness as with bloodied hands he cradled his pal's head: the times they had spent together in every kind of scrape, the lies they had spun to keep each other out of trouble, the everyday little things that make two humans pals. John's tears fell unashamedly until a voice nearby and a comforting hand on his shoulder gently urged him to one side. The medical teams had arrived but George was gone, his body moved no more, not even the spasmodic twitching that would give John a glimmer of hope. That too had left him, and now he was at peace. This friend would rest for eternity never to be troubled again by girl-stealers, by wars, by anything. They lifted George's body – so unconcerned by it all – they had lifted hundreds like him. To the medics yes, but to John no. This was a precious cargo, not another body for the meat wagon, this was his George. John ran towards the stretcher and cursed the bearers: "You dirty bastards, take him easy."

"Steady, son, we're only doing our job." Only doing their job. This job they did, it must surely make them into robots, seeing dying men all the time. They must have no feelings, but they would have feelings for this one, he would see to that. John's curses mounted; he saw the medics as ogres and he ran at them, fists flailing. They lowered George's body to the ground and pinned John down. "Steady, boy. Steady up there." Their voices seemed to come from a long, long way away. John struggled and kicked and fought them, but it was to no avail. His body weakened and above him stood Corporal Kane and Logie. "Stand up soldier!" The sharp yet kindly command came from the Captain. John arose instinctively to his feet; their eyes met, and in that brief look John knew that the Captain felt for him in his misery. The bearers once more bent down, and this time gently picked up their burden and went on their way. John's eyes followed them until they were out of sight and then he murmured: "So long my old son."

6

The explosions had ceased. Someone had taken care of the death-dealing mortar gunners, and at that moment John was wishing them the cruellest of deaths. He gulped air into his lungs, his mind numb; he just did things in a mechanical way. He found himself following the nearest person ahead of him, not knowing where they might lead him, just blindly going with the pack. To be with them was blind instinct; to be alone, to be away from the main herd, was to court disaster. The loner was always the one they picked off first, and although John just wanted to be left alone, he also knew it would be like those explorers who suddenly found that they were falling asleep in the snow.

Hogarth drew alongside John. "Come on son, this way. He's away from it all now." Yes, he was away from it all, but for John, a bitter lonely sickness was creeping over him, a feeling of utter depression. He stared at Hogarth, but his eyes saw only a soldier of a rank higher than his own, a person of respect, but not the same friend as had just gone over the hill. There are several kinds of pain, but this mental anguish John felt was savage in its intensity. It had a special brand of torture all of its own, indescribable. Time heals all wounds, but who believes at the time of its happening? John walked on like an automaton, his mind in a world of its own, and ahead of him was the image of the big fellow, cursing, grinning and happy, all rolled into one, and suddenly he was gone. John almost called out to him it had seemed so real, but reality had returned and John was with the majority of the boys. Several comforting arms were put around his shoulders and mumbled 'cheer ups' were uttered. They were said with genuine feeling from each man who knew what death meant and what it was like to lose a pal. John would treasure this moment forever in his memory, for it showed that human values are not all false. At home some people would go to a funeral looking sorry but not always were their true emotions exhibited, but here, amid violent death, true human kindness broke through and brought with it a ray of hope through the sadness that enshrouded him. John saw now that life could, and indeed must, go on. While men like these inhabited the earth there would be other friends, there would be other games and scrapes to get out of, there would be someone else who would lie and cheat for him. Although strictly off the record, all these were the wiles of rogues and vagabonds, they were all part of army comradeship as necessary as the generals themselves, as much a part of life as praying, eating and sleeping, they formed part of the make-up of the creatures God had placed on earth, and without these facets man was a lost cause.

John felt better now that the initial shock was over and he knew the only thing he could do was to reconcile himself to the fact that George was no more. It would not be easy, nor would it be in minutes, hours or days, but inevitably it would come to him, and the truth that time heals all would in the end prevail. But even as John pushed this age-old saying into his brain, he knew that for ever there would be that little place for George till his own breath left his body, and that the pain would be here for an eternity. Friends were hard to come by, real friends were like gold. There were others, but the nod of the head, the knowing wink, the old favourite curse, the silly saying, the stupid laugh, they were all things that only two real pals would make anything of, and a piece of metal manufactured in some foreign land had ended all the meaning of those little things in a few seconds.

John had not taken much notice of anything else in his grief over George, but now he saw others, some badly wounded, others gone for ever, people rushing and calling for people, a scene from some painting in a devil's domain; only the sickness of mankind was here, and yet out of that sickness came compassion in tender words to some dying comrade, the helping hand, the canteen of water, so even in this stinking carnage there was hope. This he knew was the first severe mauling, and in his heart John felt it was not to be his last. He also realised that manhood was being thrust upon him, not by choice but from necessity. To survive what had just been experienced, one either became a man or lay down and became a subject of scorn by those who had trodden the path before. He thought over the advantages and disadvantages of both courses, and finally it boiled down to the logical conclusion that basic training had instilled into him: that one becomes a man whether one wants to or not. There was no army regulation decreeing this, but God, you were not playing the game if you went the other way. No, he would become a man for himself.

John knew the majority expected this of him and he was too much of a coward to defy convention. All the books he had read as a youngster had a hero that usually died holding the fort single-handed; all were real men, or so the reading had implanted in his mind, so he would try to emulate those heroes. He would stand four-square to the wind, he would not run from the wretched situations in which he would find himself. He would hand himself over to others' teachings, knowing full well that he was sacrificing freedom of thought, the very thing they had said he was fighting for, and for what reward? The reward of others higher up saying "well done old chap, that's the stuff! Just the type we need", but in their hearts they had fear, and theirs was a greater fear than his because they carried an insignia on their shoulders that decreed no backing out. For them it would be a tragedy, the family disgraced, something the peasant class seemed to have no worries about. To them, perhaps, a "damn poor show" was sometimes enough to send them reaching for the family revolver.

John felt a wave of sympathy for these people, for they must have at one time faced his present situation and had made their choice, which nothing could now alter, and now that he, John, had decided to join their ranks, there was no other way for him; he could never be that odd man out and he would swell the ranks of the majority. Another conquest for the establishment. The fight would go on whether he joined them or not, so he surrendered himself to convention, or whatever man chose to call everyday happenings.

From now on life must for him take on a new meaning. This was to be a fight in which one side would survive, and as an Englishman it was to be his side. To hell with everything else, he must be on the winning side. There was no glory for the loser, only the scorn on the side-lines awaited the vanquished; much better to go home to the plaudits for the conquering heroes than the thumbs down for the defeated gladiators. John knew this now, and from this point onwards he must dedicate his efforts to winning, comforted by the thought that he could find no better comrades anywhere than those who so completely surrounded him. These boys who once trod the path he was now on were men, forged by fire and death as he had been. There were still the odd men out among them, but they too would find their moments of truth and their choice would, in the end, be the same as his own. Night and day he would have one aim: to finish the job he had been trained to do and get over this chapter of his life that had turned sour on him.

The following day arrived swiftly for John. It was Sunday, and in an old barn the chaplain called together the religious, the doubting, the unbelievers and the duty-bound. Gathered together, they rendered some of the old faithful hymns most reverently, the religious from sheer belief, the doubting in the thought that it may be true, the unbelievers just joining with the majority and the duty-bound because it was dutiful. John joined in the singing because the voices raised in unison gave a certain amount of comfort. It also seemed delightfully unreal. Here they were, singing the praises of some distant God who allowed all this slaughter, and yet, somehow, he could not join the unbelievers' brigade. The singing stopped, the chaplain raised his eyes towards heaven, and in clipped military style he offered a prayer to the Almighty, half-pleading but with a slight tone of authority. The boys had their heads bowed in reverence; even the hard guys who in civvy street would kick your teeth in if you mentioned that they had been to church bent their heads with the rest of the flock, and John felt that everybody present was helping to wing the message heavenward in a form of express delivery. A few more hymns, a few more prayers, and then it would be back to the old occupation in life of killing or of being killed. What hypocrisy this all was really! Praying to a God to whitewash your conscience; to get on with the killing with a sense of righteousness. Yet John had joined the band only a short time ago and he knew that this must be part of the way towards victory somehow, somewhere, sometime, and as long as any kind of hocus-pocus helped him to win and get out of this place he would join the movements of the hypocrites. As he once more raised his eyes to the lone figure of the chaplain in front of him, John was glad the sentries outside were giving the Lord a hand by keeping a sound watch and an all-seeing eye on the cause of delivering them from all evil.

The service ended and the men filed silently out of the makeshift church, their faces expressionless. What was going on in their minds was anyone's guess. Some were surely pinning their faith on the Lord's ability to look after them; others preferring a strong hand on the rifle butt. John drifted along following the main flow of humanity, hardly knowing where it was headed at that moment. In his mind he turned over some of the remarks made by the chaplain. To him that man was a true believer, and even though he dished it out in a soldierly manner it appeared to be something he really believed in and he seemed the happier for it. Was religion anything? Did someone up there look down with an all-seeing eye? A thousand questions to be asked, but for how long had this God allocated one's life on earth to find the answers? Still, deep down John did have an uncomfortable, odd feeling when he attempted to reflect upon it in its entirety.

Church was now behind him and he had been marching alone at a steady pace for some time. Ahead, the solitary figure of the officer stood out as a man apart. Why was it that these men seemed to stand out from the rest? Perhaps it was because of their bearing, but then they do state that guards stand as straight as ramrods. No, it was just something else John could not quite grasp. Class. Was that the description? But then again he would not admit to such a decision as, stripped naked, all men are equal. Anyway, who cared about all that really? A piece of shrapnel or a mortar bomb recognised no barriers, and at present the man up front was the prize Charlie as he carried the can for everybody. John would therefore follow and follow until the end of time, because he knew that this must be the way for he was not cut out to be the man up front.

7

The next few days seemed to pass quickly, a skirmish here and there, the living passing into the land of the dead. The everyday happenings of the soldier at war: civilians gazing in awe at the marching columns, the dead animals, the crying of women, the white-faced children, the shell-ridden countryside, the empty houses, scattered belongings, the child's doll, war's confetti strewn about like giant snowflakes, drawn faces seeking something that seemed to fade out of sight.

As the endless miles were covered, weeks passed and John began to harden as time sped by. He hardly glanced at the bodies by the roadside anymore; the sight of blood was not half as difficult to bear. A village lay ahead and from a distance looked peaceful enough, but experience had taught him that danger lurked behind all points of the compass. The officers had called their men to a halt and a conference began; no doubt discussion of their entry. Orders were shouted soon thereafter and the men split into three groups, which began to converge onto the target ahead. They were soon in the village and discovered that the Jerries had already left, but John was pleased that this prize had fallen into their hands without a struggle.

Civilians began appearing from their hiding places, some of them raising a weak cheer, and this John knew was more from relief than for conquering heroes. He glanced at the faces of the passing people and saw the misery that war was bringing etched on each one of them. They began to become less timid and to stretch out their hands to grasp the soldiers nearest to them, some with tear-stained faces, some with blank stares. A girl approached John with arms outstretched and snatched hold of him. She wept on his shoulder and John gently lifted her tear-stained face and looked into her eyes. She was pretty, but not beautiful. A few years older than he was, John estimated. She still held on to him and they both had an understanding that the war and hate were to be forgotten and not because of any love for the victory, but just for wanting to get away from all cruel things. This woman was offering herself to John so that they could share some moments of happiness – of love – and to abandon care and worry. John also felt this need and slowly the two of them edged their way to an abandoned house, soon to be locked in each other's arms letting the world as it was drift aimlessly by. She waved a shy hand as John left her, and half-embarrassed, he waved back. It was funny: there was no real love between them, but still John felt a little guilty, as though he had taken advantage of a situation and forced himself upon her. This was not so, but the feeling remained. As John walked off, he could see that some of the others had also found solace in the arms of these complete strangers. On reflection, this was not taking advantage of a situation; it was just a moment of complete peace found in the midst of strife and its common misery.

John knew that these people were their friends, but who knew, tomorrow they could be their foes. A bloody smack from Jerry and the same heroes of today could be the subject of jeers tomorrow, as they retreated. Life was just that way: neither side could give feasible solutions as to why they could occupy strangers' lands. The diplomats and government officials would always find reasons, but what do the peasants think? To help them does one blast the other's home away? To feed them does one destroy the other's livestock and churn up their arable land? To clothe them...? In a land of sun, the peasant's needs are meagre and yet these are the everyday needs of the worker, and still armies come and go throughout the ages. They come as conquerors and sometimes as the vanquished but the poor are left with no answer to their questions, and the welcome extended by these poor folk today could be their wrath of tomorrow because there is no answer to the present. Their questions would go on and on until one day there would be no shells and no killings, and the strangers would all depart and the land would heal its own wounds. The cattle could bear their young and the answers would all unfold to even the simplest minds, so simple the answers and yet so many stupid obstacles in the way to their realisation.

The village had been left behind some hours previously and they were on their way to new conquests or defeats. John had begun to accept this mode of life as though he had never known any other. Up and move, bed down, stay a night, move on, fight, relieve the nerve-shattering tension of fear, the relief of finding yourself still alive, poison, followed sometimes by the antidote for some, for others, no remedy. One's whole being just soaked up the punishment and either rejected it in the form of a breakdown or just kept on soaking it up. The bomb-happy types went off into a little world of their own, free from the outside terrors but haunted from within, by their own subconscious. Nevertheless, press on; someone's got to give way first. The fat politicians would still wear their frowns, victory or defeat. It's the money that counts. What about the communist doctrine? Karl Marx in full voice: "That's not the kind of chap we want old man, not quite the thing, you know." Who cared what doctrine – Marx or Jesus Christ – as long as they finished this bloody madness?

The trudge of marching boots alongside him brought John back to the present. It was Hogarth. "How is it keeping, son?"

"Not bad," replied John.

"That's the stuff, keep it up!" Hogarth marched off, a quiet word here, a bit of information there, morale drill thought John. But needless to say, a word of comfort at the right time did have its good points. Another rest, hard-tack biscuits out, gnaw the bloody things till they became soft. A tin of the old Maconochie Stew and a glance at the mysterious tin of emergency rations every infantryman carries. Everyone knew what its contents were: one solid lump of dehydrated-looking chocolate; and yet, this tin was regarded by most with a sort of reverence. Still, it's wonderful what one's stomach will take.

The roar of a dispatch rider's noisy bike broke the silence. A quick salute, some papers handed over, and he was gone. Captain Logie studied the papers and after a while his face broke into a smile. It must be good news, thought John. Logie made his way towards the largest group of men and signalled the rest to gather round.

"Now listen chaps, here's the best news we've had for months. The second front in Europe has opened and is going well. Our boys were parachuted over the Seine and everything seems to be going according to plan."

A spontaneous cheer broke out and John felt a curious thrill go through him. So someone else would now find his troubles beginning; please God, let them be small troubles. John let his thoughts wander to the fresh faced boys who were now going through some of his own earlier moments, but to him this was a positive sign that the war was not going to stagnate into a kind of stalemate that would go on indefinitely. There would obviously be more slaughter of innocents, but it would hasten the end one way or another. The outcome of victory was not ever sure, but amidst all John's confused thinking he hoped that the victory would be on his own side.

But there was still his own threshold of conflict to be settled and this was the concern of his immediate future: to help his superiors and comrades smash their way to victory this side of the fence. Still, this really heartening news caused a surge of hope to swell within him. The mood of most of the others became jubilant and John imagined everyone beginning to think victory to be just around the corner. But he himself preferred to reserve judgement. There was still a rocky path to be trodden and the Japs were still very much in evidence. Nevertheless the burden now would no doubt feel a lot lighter.

"On your feet, boys!" They were off again. The break always seemed to terminate so swiftly the men moved on as though drawn by some invisible magnet, pulling them towards a destiny they were never really sure of. John's feet caught the rhythm of those around him and in solitude they pushed silently onwards. John's thoughts suddenly reverted to George. The poor big old fellow had been gone some time now and by Christ he missed him badly. He would have liked to have heard George comment on this new development, as in his dry way he would have sorted out the pros and the cons of the situation. But John knew that this could only be a passing memory, as by now the poor sod was a decaying hulk returning to the dust from whence he came. It was all so strange - this life. One minute a laughing human being, the next a creature of pity with death's icy grip about its throat. Such a person commanded sympathy from everyone, even those who, in life, had never spoken to him. It seemed that death, bitter as it was, was the only thing that unifies all human souls because of the knowledge that it is inevitable and has to visit one and all. And in the dying man the onlooker sees someone who is discovering the true answer a little sooner than he himself. There also seemed to be some kind of reverence about it all but at the same time there was the awe-inspiring feeling that there was no return even if it was found that the answer was not to your liking, and only if there was a God who looked after you would you ever know whether your end was ultimate or you were the victim of the greatest fraud ever known.

Crash! John's thoughts were rudely interrupted by the sound of a mortar shell exploding nearby. God, they were in trouble again. John hugged the ground instinctively. He half lifted his head and glanced round to see what the other boys were doing. He saw Hogarth running towards him in a half-crouch. Two of the other boys were close behind him. "Follow me!" Hogarth spat out, and John joined the trio not knowing what was happening. They moved forward about 50 feet and went straight to ground again behind a smallish wall.

"Now listen", Hogarth ordered, "we think the house further up the road is held by the Jerries and the mortar gunner is around somewhere. We're going in to clear the house." He peered furtively over the wall and after a quick survey joined them again. "We're lucky! There's cover all the way to the house but there'll be a few swift sprints in between. Keep your heads down and when I give the word, follow me... Now!"

They scampered over the wall like rats, a quick sprint and down again, this time into a dip in the ground that automatically became their shelter. Funny, John thought, he was out of sight in this dip, but he felt safer behind the wall. Again Hogarth took stock of their next move. "This time lads, it's a longer run and the most open one, so watch out. Let's go." They all moved faster, inspired by the urgency in Hogarth's voice, but this time their journey was interrupted by the staccato sound of a Spandau machine gun. It spewed a stream of deadly lead towards them and a sudden whimpering sigh marked the end of another 'soldier of the king'. He just fell dead amid the flying boots of three of his brethren who were scrambling towards his killers like avenging angels. They reached their next sanctuary with one less man. They glanced at each other; no words were necessary, no prayers were said, one 'soldier, army, for the use of' was dead. John noticed that Hogarth looked a little pale and realised that no doubt the man himself was as pale as he was. The other chap, also grim-faced and tense, crouched with them.

"One more hop, boys, and those bastards will be blown sky high," Hogarth foresaw. "There's an outhouse just near the door of the main objective. Make a dash for that and once there we'll deal with them. Good luck boys."

The words bit deep into John's mind and then the words "let's go!" were heard. They sounded so uncertain, so ominous in a situation like this. Good luck, or goodbye? Soon John would know, for Hogarth was getting into position to start sprinting. A sudden "let's go", and they sped off on the last stage. The sharp banging of the Spandau started after a few feet; a scream like a wounded animal rent the air. John half-turned but a quick shout of "leave him alone" came from Hogarth, and their luckless companion joined the ranks of the dead. The outhouse was reached and John felt himself instinctively move closer to Hogarth. They were both gasping for breath from their exertions and needed a moment's pause to recover.

Hogarth, his face set, began to brief John: "Listen, son", he said, "you're safe here for now. I'm going to make a dash past the window at the side of the house. It's bound to draw the fire of their gunner, so when you hear it chattering, dash to the window by the back door of the house and sling your grenade through. Understand?". John nodded and with a grim smile Hogarth added: "And don't forget to pull the pins out." John tried to force a smile in response, but it was not forthcoming. Hogarth gripped his arm fiercely. "I'm going now, boy."

"Good luck," John said and half held Hogarth's hand. He watched as Hogarth took a deep breath. He admired this man immensely, not for him the easy task of waiting to give the coup de grâce. He had taken the role of the clay pigeon – a part he could have easily given to John, owing to his superior rank. Surely a real and courageous act from a soldier and a real man.

Now the moment had arrived. John watched tensely as Hogarth sped off, making for a small wall just beyond the side window. The Spandau began almost immediately and John dashed towards the back door. The grenade in his hand became a symbol of death and he found an excitement mounting within his breast that seemed to have an essence of evil about it. There he was, poised, with the means of life or death in his hand. To take out the pin was justice for the wrong-doer. At the same time, he wondered whether he could salve his conscience afterwards by naming the judge who had given him permission to execute this act of death. Would it be God or Man, or perhaps himself? But then, he thought, you never name yourself; there is always someone higher to carry the blame. But this choice was made and the pin was out. It flew through the window and John felt evil spread throughout his body – a feeling that Satan had won his battle against the Lord and this was his victory celebration. John crouched lower. One, two, three, he lost count and then the roar told him that there was no holding back now. The choice had been made; his hands were no longer bloodless. Another crash as the second grenade went in, and again the roar as it exploded. There was no George now to turn to and ask for reassurance. He stood alone, and during those few moments John felt the presence of malevolence together with a feeling of betrayal of all decent instincts within himself. Dear God, hold my hand. It's dark.

The dust from the explosion billowed out of the house like a flour sack that had split at the seams. John could see grey uniforms in the mist; one had a gun in his hand, which cracked as if by some unseen influence, and a body lay stiff. The kill supreme had been made. Death, this time, in sight of his own eyes and done by his own hand. Not the kill from afar by the shell or grenade, but the actual act of pointing directly and committing legalised murder. A mounting feeling of power welled up inside him. He controlled man's life and gave him his sentence, all in a few moments. Almighty judge, but was he right? Who would answer his plea: the Establishment or Almighty God? From the former he feared no judgement, from the latter he would have to wait.

Casting aside his uncertainties, John edged to the side to which Hogarth had run, but the brave NCO had not quite made his goal. Hogarth's body lay twisted and blood-stained, mouth agape, with a glazed look of bewilderment in his eyes, and now John was alone. He felt an inward sense of panic take over. How many avengers were still within the house? How many eyes were seeking out the deadly bomber? John gripped his rifle a little tighter and became concerned for his own preservation. He would surely kill again and again if necessary. He reached a door that swung crazily on its hinges. A mad dash and he was inside the house. There was an eerie silence all round him and in the far corner of the room were two grey-clad bodies ripped beyond recognition, with a Spandau gun that would never fire again. Spurred on by the sight of his minor victory, John went from room to room becoming more and more confident as each room yielded to his feeling of total victory. He found another two bodies in the back room. The end was in sight. A quick rush upstairs, with caution thrown to the wind. Empty. John had won, or rather his team had outplayed the opposition at a cost dear to both sides. He stood for a full five minutes, drinking in his triumph — a feeling of being the king of the castle as in the games of his childhood. But at the back of his mind nothing could wipe out the feeling that this game lacked the purity and cleanliness of those far-off days. The dead here would never be able to stand up and play again.

He rushed back out into the fresh air, away from the house of death. Reverently he took the Very pistol from Hogarth's body. The Very light hurried heavenward and John knew that his comrades would know of his victory. He sat down. A feeling of absolute exhaustion had come over him; his hands shook and his whole body began to follow suit, and he burst into an uncontrollable fit of weeping. Soldier triumphant? Mighty victor? Suffer little children to come unto me? How are the mighty fallen! Through tears of confusion he saw his mother, her arms outstretched.

The rest of the men were by now at his side but he had hardly noticed their arrival, and with hurried steps and a bit of back-slapping they trooped into the house. John glanced up to find Logie looking down at him. "Well done soldier! Cheer up!" They were carrying Hogarth gently away and John half rose to help them, but his legs were too weak and his hands trembled, so he just remained seated.

The weeks seemed to fly by after that incident and John found that he was regarded with affection by nearly everybody and also they thought that he was somewhat of a hero. To him, it was an ever-recurring nightmare of the mind, but at that present moment, John's thoughts dwelt on a rumour flying about among the boys to the effect that they were soon to be pulling out again and that the division was bound for duties in the Middle East. A rumour that gave considerable comfort to each man as they were all hoping it to be true. A few more days passed with the rumour growing stronger, and with the mysterious army grapevine at work the boys seemed to know as much as the commanding officer. At last it came out officially, or more or less so. They were, according to the CO, going to another sphere of operations. The mood of the men was one of jubilation and relief; a feeling that a black cloud was passing and that the eternal silver lining was about to reveal itself. These were their conversations: the farmers among them started mentioning the spring lambs; the family men dug out photographs, tattered and grimy; the single boys were already lying in the grass with a bird at the local park, and a general air of living permeated their thoughts. The fears of yesterday were slowly being vanquished by the thoughts of tomorrow and what it would bring: a cosy atmosphere; a warmth the likes of which had not been with them for months.

8

The Middle East. Flies, heat and latrines, weevils in their bread, the first impressions of a strange country, but there was also peace of mind, no bombs, no shells, no feeling of a lurking enemy. This was Palestine, and the only enemies were the Jew who lured your miserable few mills out of your pocket for an inadequate return of goods and the Arab with promises of his sister for extortionate gain for himself. But above all, there was peace, a feeling that the darkness was over, that life still had a chance, and the strained faces of the boys were beginning to show a relaxation not seen before.

John was in Haifa and the battlefields were miles away; he had money in his pocket and the beer was warm. He was alone but that did not matter: the bar offered a friendly atmosphere and the hostesses were busy soliciting their clients. She came over to him, her swaying hips almost advertising her profession. John gave her the 'come hither' look because he felt that tonight there was freedom in the true sense of the word. Her arms were twined round his neck; she was sitting on his lap whispering about a drink; his hands were around her waist; she was warm and human and the beer spurred his lust. A signal to the waiter, the expensive drink, the touch of her lips on his forehead all helped to allay his worries. Who cared about the cost of this comfort? She was woman, the ultimate aim of man, a creature to be loved and cherished; fiancée or old bag, what was the difference? She held a power over him, he loved her now, and perhaps for the next hour she belonged to him at a cost (or perhaps just a few miserable pounds in a foreign currency). His hands began to wander and she chided him for his boldness in front of the audience, who was no doubt amused at the antics of a drunken Tommy. But John cared not for their amusement; she was his prize and every penny would go on her to see that she worshipped him alone. The slightly embarrassed look told him he was going too far, but John hardly heeded the danger signal and continued to fumble and maul her, oblivious to the stares of the general public. She sensed the urgency of the occasion and smiled at him, a hurried look at the manager, a resigned look back from him, and she began leading him out of the bar to a haven provided for emergencies such as this one. She half fell onto the bed giggling and pretended to put up a show of resistance, but what a sham! John had learned the wiles of women by now and he played the game with her. He chased and she retreated, but the hunter always won in the end. His panting body finally pinned her down to the bed, which was her place, and the months of agony and terror exploded in a moment of ecstasy with this fleeting old whore. Then suddenly, John pushed her away from himself. She had become an instrument of his lust gone stale, just another means of satisfying this lust. He had paid, she had made her commission, she meant nothing to him – just another old tom who he had laid, no real love, no nothing, no future, no fondness, just another old whore to put in his books and chalk up another conquest en route to the ultimate end of life's learnings. How callous and yet how necessary in the art of living.

She was gone and he was back in barracks among a chattering crowd of drunken beer-soaked warriors all trying to relate their night's experiences at once. John listened half-amused at some of them, but through his drunken haze he saw the face of George, dear pal, gone but not forgotten. John wanted to stand up and scream for them to be silent and share his sorrow, but he knew it would be to no avail. George was just a goner to these morons and yet to John he was real again, standing there moaning about the army, boasting about the women. Tonight he would have been proud of John, and that knowing wink and the upturned thumb would have surely indicated total victory. Curse the lot of them; they did not care a damn for his sorrow. He flung off his clothes and slid into bed, their voices growing distant. To hell with the lot of them! Thoughts of a woman floated before him, George, the army, the alcohol, green fields, the city, civvy clothes, a wife, two kids, a house, a crash of bombs, the screams of men, the moans of resignation, the end of time, God, Satan, and eventually sleep blotted out all these fantasies.

A restless night, then morning with a blurred head, a stale mouth, dog tired, a realisation that the pocket was somewhat lighter, a feeling of acute embarrassment, a bawling sergeant – all the ingredients of the morning-after-the-night-before. Still, this was not the first time he had experienced this, and at least there was no one waiting to blow your head off. The sun was not giving out much heat at the unearthly hour of six, and for the next few hours they could imagine they were back in England.

Days were spent in a haphazard fashion, manoeuvres of the day and night variety, fashioning the camp in true British Army tradition, which included all the stray and mangy dogs in the area being made into pets by various soldiers, the employment of a char boy (a local Arab boy), finding the local tailor who would buy spare drill suits, the odd black-market merchant who would buy anything from a tank to a round of ammo, scouting around the perimeter of the camp for local maidens who would willingly accept invitations to tent parties after the orderly officer had done his rounds, digging latrines, thieving cocoa, and in general making life just that little more comfortable. For the present, it was drill parade. Of all the stupid chores, this was the winner. The platoon marched aimlessly about to the bellowings of a burly NCO who had no more interest in the proceedings than the men had, back and forth the only thing they got from it were sore feet and constant moans from those lads taking part. No one could understand why soldiers with line experience should have this indignity thrust upon them. Still, all the moaning in the world never altered this standing procedure and John learned to live with it.

At breakfast a sample of the local bread was again full of weevils. Either one had the bread or a form of square biscuit that was so hard that anyone with poor teeth had to settle for the bread with weevils or just go hungry. A few of the boys swore that this was part of a gigantic army plot to save rations. There was also the eternal porridge as well as the ever-faithful tinned bacon with enough fat in it to put even the biggest glutton completely off his food, and the tea was not exactly mother's. The sight of the ever-beaming smile of the complaints officer made one feel downright ashamed to question the origin of this fine fare, even though many a curse was uttered on swallowing the filth. John had not yet heard of anyone dying of any strange malady caused by the food, but at the same time this did not seem to improve its taste.

Today was to be a day of manoeuvres on a grand scale. The CO of their regiment had met his brother, who was also a CO of another infantry regiment, and they had decided to play soldiers together and the one's mob was to chase the other's. This involved galloping about up and down mountains, sleeping in holes in the ground, umpires saying "you're dead!", undelivered rations, silly bayonet charges, lashings of marching, plenty of uttered "that's not cricket old man", and a feeling of what's the use of it all. They were on parade, preparing for this great treat while the CO was busy bubbling with enthusiasm. They were to prove to his brother Cedric (or was it Fred?) that they were a superior team, and by God, anyone who let the side down would jolly well pay for it. Nodded heads from crony officers signified that nasty punishment awaited the defaulters. The mess of khaki-clad figures accepted this because there was no superior judge to whom they could appeal and so it was that John, after an hour's solid footslogging, found himself up one of those steep mountains, staring down into the valley below. Taffy, alongside him, was in raptures, muttering about life back home in the valley. Below there was nothing in the shape of brother Cedric's men except another ominous-looking mountain on the other side; it was obvious enough to even the dimmest of men that this peak would also have to be conquered. And what then? Would brother Cedric's men be found? If they did, John hoped for a quick capitulation, or for that matter, his lot would surrender and risk the eternal wrath of Basil (or was it Rodney?).

111

John's guess was right – they were slogging their way up the other side, and if Cedric's men were there, they would willingly strangle all of them to give victory to the home side. This was not to be. The army does not play it that easy. One has to rough it first before one gets the cake, and it was not for days that battle commenced, by which time every man was a potential deserter, making the task of the umpires twice as difficult. Nights of bedding down under one's army gas cape does not help one's temper, and John was no exception. He felt miserable, but they had caught up with the elusive prey and men were being declared dead all over the place, some because of the physical fatigue the umpires were in and others purposely throwing themselves in the paths of mythical tanks or dashing straight into a battery of artillery fire, and as far as Victoria Crosses were concerned, they would have run out of the metal from the Balaclava guns long ago.

The game had come to an end and it was back to barracks by trucks. John's feet were killing him and the sight of the trucks was a blessing. The CO was walking about with the look of a man who had just stopped Napoleon at Waterloo and no doubt would write home to Penelope telling her all about his gallant exploits amongst the thunder flashes. He would toast his victory in the mess, and John could see him as he would describe the advance: a handful of salted peanuts taking the place of the infantry, the salt cellar becoming the tank, the vinegar decanter being sent flying across the table as the salt cellar gave it a full blast with its gun, and the whisky-guided hand raised in a gesture of triumph. Good luck to him. The boys would also celebrate in beer their release from the mock battle. The dust poured into the back of the trucks as they sped down the road, and the boys began to sing, which was always a sign that Tommy Atkins had again won through.

The next few weeks were a mixture of the same formula. The boys had established quite a good bartering system with the local spivs, and a series of mysterious bottles of potent liquor were finding their way into the tents at night; many an unconscious body was to be found lying in the company lines. Several local Arab gentlemen were to be seen walking about looking very much like British soldiers in their khaki drill shirts and trousers, several also sporting army boots a couple of sizes too large. It was also rumoured that the old woman of 50 plus who did the boys' laundry was quite a good sport, and many a lad had already introduced himself to some of the local bints who crept about so mysteriously. In this respect John did not have much luck, although perhaps some of the other boys were a little more industrious than he was. The local orange orchards were ceremoniously raided day and night, and they always managed to have a large supply of eggs on hand, so life was just about coming round to their way of thinking and it would not be long before an illicit still would be born in the camp, cutting out the greedy middleman. There was also Shaftoe's cinema, a place of entertainment with no roof, films which started and cut out after the first few minutes, restarted, only to break again amid the jeers of the watching boys. The lads had also found a way of avoiding paying their ackers to get into this flea-pit. They simply printed the name of the cinema on old chewing gum wrappers, and in the weary torchlight of the Arab usherette it was an exact replica of the real thing.

Beirut, city of sin in the Lebanon, was the place chosen by the majority of the boys in which to spend their leave. Not that they had much choice. It was to be either there or Jerusalem, and as most of them knew that Beirut offered the lot, John chose this place too, but because it was a city of excitement in every way. Cairo had its places as did Alexandria, but Beirut incorporated everything they had into one. There was Susie's bar, the Kit-Kat Club, the dirty out-of-bounds area where one's throat was in danger of being slit if one walked alone, the legitimate brothel staffed by medically-inspected women – it was at this place that most of the boys spent their leisure and it was here that John found himself heading for. The place was small in comparison with the number of soldiers it accommodated, but here was life in the raw. The hardened womaniser, the dirty old man, the shy kid on his first round-up, the sadistic pervert – every vice practised and accepted by a staff of experienced old whores. There was even a photographer on duty who was willing to take photographs of the actual act.

By the time John strode in most of the boys were already there, some with women sitting on their laps and being tuned up for the revelry to follow. Already trouble had brewed when a drink-maddened Scot soldier had rushed one of the birds out of the room onto the balcony and tried to snatch the goods without paying, and proving, once and for all to the onlookers that the true Scot wears nothing under his kilt! John duly paid the old hag at the door for the small ticket that entitled him to any one of the girls on duty and joined a bunch of other lads who were busy ogling the tarts with the best credentials. "Hello, John, boy." Their voices sounded warm and friendly and gave John a good feeling. "Come on, son, join

114

the party." A tray of beer appeared and was devoured within a few seconds. Another tray followed and suffered the same fate, and it was not long before John began singing lusty and bawdy choruses of the famous filthy army songs that have chorused around the world in every fighting sphere Tommy Atkins has ever served in since time immemorial.

The boys had marked one of the shy members of the group to prove his manhood, and between them they had selected some busty Turk for him. The lad was putting up a brave show, saying he would take her when he was ready, but he could not deceive them; John knew exactly how he felt and sympathised secretly. Eventually, though, he had to carry through with his act, and amid ironic cheers from the boys, he half-staggered towards the big Turk, who smilingly led him off to one of the rooms laid on for the convenience of the customers. The boys all gazed after him and those who had had their tickets' worth fell back on their memories, while those such as John who still had the pleasure to come smiled benignly. But hello, what was this? The door of the Turk's room had opened only a few minutes after their entry and the shy boy's head was peeping round. "Hey fellows", he shouted quickly, "do I have to take my vest off?" This caused such a roar of laughter from the rest of them, that the poor lad shot straight back in, his question unanswered. A few of the boys dived over and began spying through the keyhole amid shouts of "dirty old bastards!" from the onlookers. The Madam quickly dispersed the keyhole crowd with a gentle chiding and they left the lad to get on with it.

Eventually the lad came out with the same look of triumph that John had come to know so well. They swarmed around him, all eager for the sordid details. His shyness was gone and he spilled it all out as though this was his everyday vocation. He knew that they had accepted him now, and the more lurid he could make his tale the higher the grade he would receive; from his yarn, John knew he would certainly reach the top rating.

By this time the beer had reached John's head and his ticket was not to be wasted. His eyes searched the room. There were no ravishing beauties and it was hard to say who was the most presentable, but the Syrian appeared slightly less obnoxious than the rest and John made her his choice. He casually waved the ticket at her and in a flash, right in front of the others, she was sitting on his lap with her arms around his neck and pawing away thinking of the commission on the little piece of paper he held. "You randy old sod", the chant began, and while their good-natured banter followed him, John whisked his lady-love off; the remarks that used to turn his face crimson hurt him no more.

In her room, an oriental perfume pervaded the air. She gave him a weary look and began to disrobe.

"Anything special?" she asked casually.

John pitied her. "No," he said, guilt sounding in his voice. She lay on the bed, arms outstretched, a false smile playing around her mouth – a smile she had used a hundred or more times a week; a weary, commission-taunted smile, hopeless and yet necessary in her trade. John came into her arms and for the moment all revulsion disappeared, only to return a minute later with a deeper intensity. She held onto him as he went to get up, but he

116

pushed her away angrily. She pouted as he wiped his mouth on his shirt sleeve and spat in the wash bowl. He threw his ticket on the table beside the bed and strode out without a word of thanks. She gazed after him with a resigned look. It was over, but she knew that other beer-sodden ticket holders were waiting for her.

All too soon leave came to an end and once again came boredom with the everyday routine. Also, the flies in the area seemed to have singled John out for a special vendetta. The flies simply thrived on the cream that was supposed to deter them, and came in all shapes and sizes, taking large lumps out of one's body. The heat was oppressive at times; a sweat-soaked shirt made one smell in a most objectionable way, and the tents at night were no garden of roses. John lay back on his bed in this stinking atmosphere and thought back on his earlier experiences; he at once realised its advantages compared with those of previous times, and decided it was far better to fight the flies and to smell like a polecat than to be dead.

9

Months of nothing special – a laugh, a moan at stupid rules that constantly cropped up in company orders, eternal marches, square bashing manoeuvres, the odd camp concert in which some stupid officer dressed as a woman and showed what a real queer he was to the shame of his fellow brethren. "Tut tut, not in front of the men." Sentry duty at night to the howls of jackals fighting over the contents of the camp dustbins, the fly-traps full of black corpses, sand in one's eyes, socks and navels, and the food bad enough to make a true chef commit hara-kiri.

The camp was now fully in order for the boys with regard to all the fiddles one could get up to, and the illicit brewery was in full production. A series of reps from both Arabs and Jews had been sounding out the possibilities of buying arms from the boys, but this one carried too stiff a penalty to have anything to do with; besides, there was also the thought that a round of one's own ammo would end up in one's own head one day. Women were in rather short supply and rumours that old so-and-so was a bit queer seeped constantly around camp. All in all, life was not too bad.

After months of this, it was good old leave-time again and on this occasion Beirut had been cancelled out for some reason, so it was Jerusalem or nothing. Some of the lads had reputedly wept openly at the loss of this outlet – to them going to Jerusalem was not leave, but a kind of penance for their sins. John kept an open mind and waited for his own visit before giving a verdict. The lorries pulled into camp and were soon full of eager men going on leave, all taking the mickey out of the boys who were unlucky this time, and before long they were on their way passing through lush country side with lazy Arabs crouched in the sun with their donkeys burdened under impossible loads. Orange groves, vineyards, the odd flash of modern times as a new car sped past them, the choking dust, the wolf-whistle from their truck at some female forms, and then the traffic gradually beginning to thicken, houses beginning to appear more frequently; this was the outskirts of the holy city, and John instinctively felt that this place was to mean something to him.

They were approaching Jerusalem itself and heads were filling the space at the back of the lorry. At first glance it was just the same as any other large town out East, but the further they went in, the more John was struck by the majesty of the place. The old and the new seemed to blend so well. He tried to think back to Bible quotations on Jerusalem, but his knowledge of the Good Book was scant. The leave camp loomed up and they could see a row of tidy Nissen huts with the little gardens in front of them that the high commander always seemed to insist upon. In all, at first glance, a tidy place. After a time spent sorting out their huts, John took a walk around the camp. The odd empty beer bottle was evidence of the previous occupants' enjoyment. Arab boys with beaming smiles

119

went about their tasks of cleaning up, and there were the permanent British staff with God-another-lot looks all over their faces. Following tradition, John scoured the perimeter for the 'late coming-in hole', and true to form, right at the end of the camp, the barbed wire had been stretched enough to allow one person to creep in at any time. Having established all the main points, he returned to his hut. It appeared neat – even a carpet was on the floor – and the beds had real sheets. Also the mosquito nets were new – quite a change from the tattered rugs that served them back at camp. The notice board on the door decreed to all and sundry the do's and don'ts, including the eternal ending to the don'ts of 'prejudicial to good military discipline', a stock phrase meaning 56 days in the glasshouse if you were foolish enough to disobey. Mind you, there were ways of wangling one's way out of some of the most diabolical situations. It boiled down to being a prince of liars and John smiled to himself as he gazed at the list of don'ts and thought of Taffy who held the crown in the regiment.

Taffy had once been found drunk and disorderly and, on being charged, had spun the greatest ever yarn to the CO. He claimed that on the day of his offence, he had embraced the Mohammedan faith, turning from Church of England overnight, and the reason he was drunk was that on the day in question, it was the feast of Mohammed. The CO had taken kindly to this outrageous story and Taffy had got away with a ticking off. At the same time he took the crown from the previous wearer, who had successfully pleaded that he had been fighting seven Arabs for the honour of the regiment. This was an old story but the man's eloquence had swayed the CO into believing it – definitely no mean feat.

A note caught John's eye. There would be a few vacancies on the pilgrimage to Bethlehem. Anyone wishing to go was to write his name on the list. John took out his pen and then hesitated. Strange to say, hardened now though he was, he thought for the moment of the reaction of the others at seeing his name on this list and the sarcastic ridicule it might bring. Comments such as: "He's gone all holy Joe" and "It's in the brothels not the manger." It was only momentary. John printed his name boldly and promptly walked off. The trip was to be on Christmas Eve, just two days off, and he would go because he felt somehow compelled to do so from within.

Early the next day, on his own, John went downtown, not like old times this, because George was absent. He walked around just looking at the sights: the modern part of this city, the lovely King David's Hotel and the dirty side of Jaffa. The bars here were plush, and Jewish ladies made it plain to Gentile gentlemen that their attentions were not welcome. Also, Palestine police were in abundance, so altogether it added up to a very civilised community, alas not to every soldier's liking. John spent the day there quite pleasantly having an odd drink here and there and a sumptuous meal, although this certainly cost him plenty. The place looked beautiful at night with neon strips contrasting with the ancient sights; colourful dresses of the modern Jewesses and the flowing robes of the wealthy Arabs; the beggars all added a touch of the mysterious East one reads about in books. There was a cold nip in the air – a sure sign that it was near going-home time. That night he would have no need of the back way in, he was all legitimate, and the following day, on to Bethlehem. John strolled casually past the sentry who seemed rather surprised that he was back so early, or rather at the regular time, as they usually turned a blind eye to those who were just a little late. Very few people were in his hut when he opened the door, and in a way John was glad as tonight he wanted to be alone. He could not shake off the small voice from afar that seemed to whisper: "Bethlehem is real." He undressed, lay back on his bed and thought of how different this place was from Beirut, the sin city, with its teeming vices and this place so quiet by comparison. John felt himself dozing off and a chorus of voices started reverberating in his mind: "Jerusalem, Jerusalem – O little town of Bethlehem."

Morning came, but this time no noisy blast of trumpets to greet him, just the sounds of the other fellows busying themselves getting ready for any ventures they had planned for that day. One could get up when one wanted to – after all this was a leave camp – and John felt relieved that no bellowing sergeant was lurking about just waiting to scream in his ear. It was around 10.00 now and tonight was the pilgrimage; until then he would saunter once more downtown and pass the time away.

The huts had been suitably festooned for the Christmas period and this time John really felt the spirit of it as he knew he was where it had all begun thousands of years ago. For some of the boys it had already begun by the sound of the bottles, and John wondered how many of them would be on their feet at the end of the day. A tug at his bedclothes brought him quickly wholly upright. It was Taffy. "Have a drink John, and all the best to you." John thanked the jolly Welshman and wished him the same as he downed the drink. "Well, I'm off," Taffy declared. "See what I can find for Christmas," and with a knowing wink he had gone. John gazed after him. There was a character if ever there was one; the king of liars now, but a damn fine soldier and the type you could always rely on to help you out in any emergency. He was certainly one who would not be sober later.

10

The pilgrimage began in an unspectacular way. There was no sense of a great occasion, just the tramp of feet of the people of many lands. There were no brass bands, no kilted pipers, no cheerleaders, just people moving towards something mysterious. Many doubters, many believers, many curious and uncommitted, but all going in the same direction seeking answers. The road was not modern, but was more a long winding path – a historic road that held John in awe. He felt that he was a minute speck of dust and that time was standing still for him, just to give him a view of all the countless feet that had trodden this path before him, and he felt so insignificant as to be ashamed in this gathering.

A slow chant started from those at the front of the column, gathering voices as it trickled down towards him: "O, little town of Bethlehem..." The words of this hymn began to mean something now and John felt no shame as his voice joined the others. This was no vulgar army duty, it had meaning, real meaning, something that had gone on for thousands of years, and as it spread throughout this throng, John felt that here was the answer he sought.

The stars above their heads had a true beauty tonight as though dressed for the occasion. His voice became more distinct as he found meaning to the words. John sang tonight not as they did in the camp chapel, half-heartedly and muttering when they were too lazy to remember the real words; tonight those words came easily and from the heart. The small town of Bethlehem itself came into view and the white houses stood out in the night. John believed that in this tiny place lay the answer to all the fears and doubts that had beset him on earth, and somehow now he did not fear the answer.

It was some time before John finally arrived at the crib, as countless others had filed in ahead of him, perhaps seeking answers as he was. He stood looking at the place where it had all begun. It was so humble and yet, amid this poverty-stricken structure, there seemed to radiate a truth that lifted all sorrow, ended all pain, gave the heart courage and the answer for which he had so long been seeking. God existed and was real. He was no man-made fairy tale. John stared hard and his doubts began to lift, not by visions, but simply by knowing that something did happen here thousands of years before his time. Men had fought and men had died, and God had been praised and cursed, and many had died never knowing the answer to it all, and for these people John felt sympathy tonight. He felt that he was one of the privileged people who had been allowed the answer to something that he could never fully understand. Even now a million questions remained unanswered to this master pattern, but to John the most important of all had been revealed and it rang round and round in his head: God existed! God was real!

The pilgrimage came to an end and men went their separate ways, some to army camps, others to their comfortable homes, others perhaps slept under the stars. All manner of people had been here tonight but all of them, John felt, would find some kind of answer. He felt happy that he had taken this wonderful trip, sensing that it had been part of his destiny. Let the others scoff at him when he relayed his story back at camp, but their scorn would be as nothing, and tell them he most certainly would. One returned from Beirut with a feeling of having had a leave of utter debauchery and was pleased with the experience, but from here there was a feeling of cleanliness, a feeling that the Master absolved one for past sins. Yes, John was glad he had gone – something to remember for ever.

He arrived back at camp to the strains of 'Good King Wenceslas' and 'The First Noel', the clink of bottles, the smell of beer, roars of laughter, to the chatter of the family man relating stories of Christmases gone by, talk of future times, the quiet one wanting to be left alone, the drunk spewing his guts up outside the door, those dead to the world whose Christmas Eve had ended, flushed faces and pale ones, all of this a patchwork quilt of humanity, a coat of many colours.

"Hello, and how's St John?" John ignored the caller; it was not a vicious question. Taffy was in the middle of the proceedings and sprang to his side. "Hello John, had a good time?"

"Yes, great," John replied quietly.

"So have I," Taffy said. "Picked myself up a lovely wog, and did I give her some." He laughed. John smiled; Taffy would always be the same, but he knew that this man would not take the mickey out of him, and he began to relay his evening's outing. Taffy listened earnestly and even mentioned the fact that he had been at chapel himself, no doubt in an attempt to atone for his feelings of guilt.

"I'm glad for you, boyo", he said eventually, "you see, I wanted to go myself, but I couldn't find the list." John smiled at this statement. Taffy was not crowned King of Liars for nothing, but he would pass it off in gratitude for his listening to him. "Well come on, Bach, and have a drink. The night is young and after all we're free men for a while yet." He pushed his way towards the crate and came back with bottles tucked under his arms, down his shirt and in his pockets. It appeared that chapel was to be forgotten and John graciously took the hint. The foam from the beer dripped down both their uniforms as Taffy poured. He would never make a barman. "Bottoms up, boyo", he said, and with a sink-like gurgle bottle number one had been demolished; at least bottle number one for John, for Taffy it looked more like bottle number 50. A huge smile lit his face as he motioned to John for his glass to be refilled with this elixir of life, and John instinctively knew that this was to go on till one cried: "Enough!"

The tinsel and glitter was dead, and morning came amid a welter of bottles strewn all over the floor; some had splintered, others lay half-empty. Some of the boys were still in their beds while others, fully dressed, lay motionless in heaps on the floor. All around him John could see the remains of the night's festivities; his own mouth felt dry and his tongue like sandpaper. The inert form of Taffy lay a few feet away, one arm under his head, the other clutching an empty bottle. John gradually began to remember how he had had to stop trying to match the Welshman at bottle for bottle the night before, and wondered how many more bottles Taffy had consumed before he had finally succumbed.

The next few days passed in similar fashion: one glorious booze-up with the odd break for meals, the forever-skints borrowing off the always-got-it types with vague promises of repayment sometime, but all too soon it was over and it was back to the grindstone.

The journey back to their own camp was very different from the outward one – the faces were thoughtful this time, no smiles of anticipation as they knew only too well what the routine would be at the end of the journey. The awful voice of the physical training sergeant must have sounded deadly in many an ear, and for others the rousing sound of reveille at six was the trumpet of death. For John it was a memorable time. Bethlehem stood out and would be for ever a precious stone in life's collection. The camaraderie of the boys over the past days also showed how enjoyable life could be when everyone showed their happy side. Bless them all, each in his turn had his good points. They were back; the gates swung open, the sentries grinning at the solemn looks as the boys leaped out of the trucks. Passing sergeants and NCOs licked their lips thinking up devilish schemes as to how to knock this beer-ravaged rabble into some kind of shape. Officers took their quivering salutes with more than usual disdain and there was a general feeling that life was about to begin again. Everyone dispersed to their own abodes to catch up on the mass of paper orders that suitably adorned their hut doors. Some who had, in pre-holiday spirits, given vent to their happiness were no doubt scanning the list of barrack room damages to see what further financial burdens they were due to bear. Others were reading the usual list of 'thou shalt nots' and 'thou shalts'; altogether a mass of formidable literature to be consumed and digested. Fortunately for John he found nothing that directly disturbed his future, though Taffy had apparently found that a chair was rather a costly article and a suitable deduction from his meagre earnings would be made towards its repair. He was giving vent to this injustice, muttering fearful sounds in Welsh that sounded as though the receiver of this tirade would find death most comforting. He bore a look of stoicism that swore that the world was on his back.

A Scot gentleman was raving about the thieving swine that had rifled a man's locker box while his back was turned and was vowing to behead the culprit. They had even taken his underpants with the holes in them – "now what use were they?" he was ranting wildly. John looked on, highly amused at these ravings although he was very careful not to show a trace of a smile the Scotsman's way as he was very near to the foaming at the mouth stage and John was sure the discovery of even another sock missing would turn the scales in favour of insanity.

Eventually all shouting ceased as the grating voice of a sergeant echoed throughout this palace of discontent, and even a servile look of discipline was restored to the eye of the mad Scot.

"Outside at the double you snivelling leave-hadders," he screamed. "I'll wake you. Shower up! Come on, let's have you!"

A mad rush and a hurried semblance of a line was formed on the square, and once more the eternal drill parades began. Up two three, down two three, saluting to the left, saluting to the right, about turn, left turn, right turn. It was a wonder no one had found a feasible reason why the order 'walking on your hands, begin' should not have been included in this repertoire. The sweat trickled down many a good man's face as the beer seeped out of pores, and pained expressions were in great evidence; resigned faces of the grin-and-bear-it brigade, the curled lips of the potential sergeant-stranglers, all boots clicking together giving no hint of their wearers' thoughts, this being the ultimate aim of the sergeant who cared not for the death sentences he knew were oft wished upon him.

It was surprising what a few weeks of this intense physical activity could do to one's physical condition, even the bleary-eyed took on a new look of fitness, and John not the least felt a much better man for it.

Manoeuvres were becoming more frequent and the idea of a move was again in the air. After a while this mysterious feeling of impending activity became commonplace among hardened sweats and it nearly always proved true, as John had discovered. This time, constant rumour was being whispered: "Europe-bound." The war was going fairly well over there and to those in the Middle East it seemed to be a war of its own – a war fought by their own kith and kin – but distinctly one in which they were not involved. As this crossed John's mind he felt a little ashamed at the selfishness of his thoughts. He felt that having fought this side of the water and given a good account of themselves, they should be (if the rumour were true) exempted from having to fight this 'private army's' battle somewhere else. But was he really ashamed of this thought, or was it in fact his innermost hope for self-preservation surging up? Either way John would go where they decreed and, after all, he had once vowed that the quicker he could finish with all this the better, no matter what the means or strategy. Still – and this was a sobering thought – although they knew that at some time they would go somewhere else, life here in the Middle East had its advantages. It was safe, selfish though it seemed, and to John a not very savoury view of the future was looming up fast.

It was but a few days later that the news was out. They were moving, and of course, again, no one was supposed to know where, but if the high-ups cared to ask the intelligentsia of the ranks, they would practically have been furnished with the full details. So, John thought, it was back to the noise and things that go bang in the night. What a position to place a human frame in, from comparative safety to a state once more of animal cunning in keeping alive. One spun a top, let it stop and then spun it again. In the olden days the top went round because one whipped it, but now they were automatic ones that whistled as they spun; no whip was needed, only a lever was pressed gently. Things had not changed much throughout the ages really; it was done in a more subtle way that was all.

Was there to be another talk on a further sphere of operations? God, not that tripe all over again. Spit out the truth, say outright that we are needed to kill some more of the bastards somewhere else and we have the transport to get you there. Please, no sugar-coated pill this time. The only difference to John on this occasion was that he had faced the real thing once and not done too badly, and that was the only comforting thought that he had at present. At the same time he knew that this provided no armour plating: death came to the inexperienced as well as to the pro. No wishes, no thoughts can alter the train of events and John knew that the only thing left was to become resigned to the future. A case once more of what will be will be; the triumphant product of the indoctrinated mind and body, the perfect thought implanted like a forced pearl grown in an oyster. Perhaps another campaign ribbon to festoon the breast and for a son to take to school and say: "Look what my Dad won." If only he were still here. Still, the medals looked pretty on the photo. How dusty that photo is, as careworn mother with tear-stained eyes gives it a flick with the feather-duster. "Must be off to work now son", she says, "mind the roads as you go off to school."

11

The move came swifter than at first anticipated and before they realised it, the men were on their way. Keep the men's minds active; give them no room to stagnate, that's the secret, for in stagnating minds come the birth of a strange kind of truth – one not quite acceptable to the hierarchy.

An apparently endless run in the trucks again produced parched throats – oh for some of those wasted bottles from Christmas! All the men were now veterans with faces more hardened, brown and hawk like after dehydration under the Palestinian sun. John blinked hard as a swirl of dust poured into the back of the truck. Curse the driver: he always took bends too sharply. An hour, two hours, an attempt at sleep was virtually impossible in this set-up. Nevertheless he must try, but it was no good. Perhaps a song would break the monotony, but who would start it? No one. Christ, what a miserable lot! A chat, but to whom? Taffy? No. He looked down in the mouth. For that matter what was there to chat about? Nothing! John left it at that and joined the ranks of the miserable.

He woke up with a start. He had achieved the impossible and had actually slept. They had arrived at the port of embarkation. Not a great liner this time; she was a converted French destroyer and at first glance really small. Cranes swung into action; all sorts of stuff was going aboard and its human cargo was starting to line up slowly as truck after truck emptied its load. The shuffle of boots could be heard. Not the same thrill this time as John joined the line-up. No more the eager kid with the wide eyes seeing this as a great adventure; this time he boarded as a man.

It was a funny ship this; it seemed to be leaning over to one side. Small down below as he had imagined, but taking plenty on board. John sorted out his corner on this floating armoury and flung his cumbersome kit onto the deck. What a relief to get rid of these articles that always seemed to hang on one at every angle! How long now, he wondered, before the familiar sound of revving engines began? Finally everything needed was aboard. No time had been wasted and they were on their way. In the dim surroundings down below John chose a bunk and swung into it. It was not like the big ship they had sailed out on; this one bucked and swayed, and he guessed that before very long sea-sickness would be his lot. Anyway, for the time being he would rest. It was strange that this time he did not seem to worry as much about his ultimate destination. He remembered his fears and doubts on the outward journey; perhaps he felt it was because he was more sure of himself on this trip. Hours passed and the first of the seasick boys had already made their trips to the latrines, returning with chalk-white faces only to rush straight back again. John, too, was nearing their state of misery and blessed the day he had changed his mind about joining the navy. He was off past snoring bunks of the lucky travellers up the iron staircase to the latrine. He just made it. His stomach knotted. Fellow sufferers were all standing alongside him. What a wretched complaint! How he envied the peaceful snorers lying so unconcerned in their bunks. After a prolonged session of back and forth and constant stomach upheavals, John's dearest wish was to set foot on dry land. Anywhere would do: a desert island, the fiercest beach-head, anywhere but not in this bucking machine!

At long last and thankfully, another destination was at hand and this was Europe, the south of France, Marseilles. Everybody was saying: "I told you so." The south of France to John was something out of story books, conjuring up visions of the almighty rich, playground of millionaires, sun-drenched beaches, wonderful suntanned girls. But this must surely be the wrong place. This port had no idle rich, no suntanned beauties lay around – just a few grim-looking dockers were the welcoming committee and the sky was full of rain. A sense of urgency again hurried unloading, and the barking of orders as batches of men came off the ship. "Quick march, left right, left right, on you go. Follow the leader, keep in line. Hurry up, wake up there! You at the back – hold your head up. Left right, keep in step, follow the leader – he knows where he's going even if you don't!"

Not far from the ship on waste ground were rows of tents, a sure sign of a short stay: a day, two days, not more, that was John's guess, but then where? How much ground had been won this side of the water? How miserably uninformed they were! No gunfire could be heard, which was a comforting thought. The tents were being filled by suntanned veterans of a war they had thought was over, but now it was about to begin again. How much more ground was to be covered before everyone called it quits? How many of these suntanned warriors would return to being pale-faced natural men again? The night was spent under canvas, with rain pattering on the tents and drips flooding in; sleep was uncomfortable and morning was welcomed. No time was wasted for the trucks had lined up in the night. They were organised here. After a hurried breakfast made by sleepy cooks, the trucks were loaded and on the men went again. Farewell playground of the rich, good-bye suntanned lady, perhaps one day she would be there when they returned again. But for now, not an opportune moment to think of her blue skies, just a one night stay – enough to tell the people back home without blushing: "I stayed in the south of France." "What hotel?" (Well, one always did forget the names of those damn foreign places!)

What a marvel the way the drivers handled the trucks, and God knows how they knew the way. Hours of gear-changing, bends, country roads, town, city, all came the same to these heroes on wheels, while their cargo just sat glumly in the back never thinking of their skill. On and on with a stop now and again for nature's requirements. They were near the end of French ground now and Belgium was the next of the signs indicating that they were not far off. The boys over here had certainly conquered some ground, much more than John had imagined. After Belgium would come the place where all this trouble originated, the Land of the Hun, the nest of savage warriors. They would have to stamp on all the eggs; perhaps it would not be easy, but John felt it possible that the end could be achieved if all went well. In terms of the ordinary soldier this meant going forward with no strategic withdrawals.

They were travelling through Belgian territory now, passing smiling faces of greetings from grateful people with friendly waves for the khaki, obviously much more welcome than field grey. They had a long stop on the outskirts of a big town where they had plenty to eat – must have been a bonus ration. A number of convoys were moving up past theirs, making one conscious of a mightier force here than in Italy. The guards flashed past, distinct snobs these boys, but admired by John and the rest. Hello Belgium, good-bye Belgium, as quickly as that, and on to the land of the tormentors. John was awestruck at the devastation the RAF had inflicted on this place. Rubble upon rubble, empty spaces and the stench of death in the air; sullen faces full of disbelief that here were the Englanders. Town, city, all alike, were pounded into nothingness. The litter of battle was apparent everywhere: the burned out tiger tank, the little British Bren carrier, guns twisted like sticks of liquorice in a child's hand, refugees of war trying to salvage some form of living from this absolute but fully deserved devastation.

Into one of these ghost towns their convoy finally rode and came to a halt in an area where the houses were least damaged; some of these were selected as billets for John's company. There are things one remembers for ever and John knew that this scene of utter chaos was to be one of those that would be indelibly impregnated into his mind. Yet he was here, no doubt, to be the instrument of adding further to this inglorious scene.

The house he was to occupy was already being searched thoroughly by the boys, not only for booby-traps but for loot as well. After all, it was the prize of any mercenary and gave spur to go on to the next objective, hoping for richer spoils. The main bed was already occupied, less a few blankets snatched by the unsuccessful rival; the old stove was slowly beginning to smoke as fuel was placed on its cold ashes; voices echoed in the deserted rooms, a tidy home once no doubt, but now in the hands of the conquerors. It never took long for old hands like them to set up camp and soon the row of houses sported a cook-house, the CO's headquarters and officers' and other ranks' abodes, and all their future now depended on orders that would be delivered to the bomb-battered quarters of the commanding officer. Theirs was not to reason why, or where, or what, but with the night fast approaching, would there be a stay of execution? Yes, they were ordered to bed down by a loud-mouthed sergeant who would most certainly win the job of town-crier. John secured a position just in front of the stove, lovely and warm there, although there was always the danger of the exploding tins of stew the boys had a habit of placing on top of it (they were always too lazy to punch holes in them first). However, you could scrape off stew more than you could scrape off shrapnel. A violent argument was going on somewhere in the house, very close to blows and all over a pillow. It seemed hardly a vital issue John thought, drowsily taking comfort in the warmth of the stove; it's going to be a comfortable night providing there are no bumps in it. The pillow dispute was settled and quietness descended. Peace on earth and goodwill to all men, or was that only said at Christmas? He wondered how much goodwill would be offered in the morning. Amid snores, deep sighs, an odd belch, the stink of rotten feet and with the fire slowly dying, John drifted into sleep.

Morning dawned, cold and grey, in the shape of Loudmouth. John's mouth felt like a sewer. The stink of feet was unbearable and the moans and groans of the boys reached fearful proportions. Get them at the enemies' throats in this mood, John thought, and it would all soon be over. Some washed and some didn't, but they all reached the cook-house with clean tins or grimy tins – all depended on what the individual's stomach would stand. To the cooks it was immaterial; it flopped in both types of container. In the middle of this slop they were informed of the parade that was to be held in half-an-hour – a parade no doubt to enlighten them on their next move, or as they termed it 'to put you in the picture', and the local schoolroom was to serve the purpose for this briefing.

There was an air of quiet before the great man arrived, a hush of expectancy and then he was there, flanked by his ever-watchful aides-de-camp. A little cough and then: "Well lads, this is it. This is where we are going to bash the Boche with all we've got." John almost laughed out loud. Coming from the cultured voice it sounded so funny. "Bash the Boche!" He had looked so earnest when he had said it, so full of enthusiasm. He continued: "You have been selected for a special task" Funny how all their tasks were special, and John wondered who did the ordinary ones. From then onward it became plain that there was to be a river crossing for them. Yankee guns would do their worst before their assault-boats took off, and then further orders would be issued. So now they knew, as if it made any difference; but for the present there was still a little time left and some of the boys were already supplementing their rations by capturing chickens that roamed aimlessly about. A Yankee convoy was passing through. Shouts of "hiya Yank", as the gum-chewing boys waved back. John began to wonder how many hours away the front line was, for there was plenty of air activity here as well, fortunately all their own markings. Very different here from Italy, where air support was scanty.

A dispatch rider arrived, his bike roaring to a halt at the CO's house. What now? Was this the coded signal to push on? They would soon know. An hour, two hours, and then "out on parade", came the orders from scurrying NCOs and once more the lorries began to assemble. This was it. They were off. The move was on them again.

Not long after everyone was in and their convoy moved off; John secured a seat at the back and looked out at the passing scenery. They travelled through a densely wooded area in beautiful countryside, then through a small village once no doubt a tourist attraction, still pretty under a cloudy sky with glum and sullen civilians. No smiles back from the Fräuleins despite persistent wolf-whistles. A screech of aircraft overhead brought John's head back into the truck. Again their own. How swift they were – over you and gone.

The convoy was slowing down at the front and his vehicle ground to a halt. Was this it? If so, it was not very noisy; in fact it seemed altogether peaceful. No, they were moving again. The cause for the delay was soon to be seen as they passed one of the trucks with its axle gone. But not too long after they again slowed down, and this time they all had to get out and were ushered off the road into the woods nearby. The trucks about-turned after unloading and were soon gone. After a rapid assembly and up through the woods for about half an hour's plod, there in front of them were the banks of a river. The men stopped for a while some four or five hundred yards before the bank itself and received hurried directions as to the allotted area for each of them, and then the "dig in" command. Curse these small shovels, although the earth was soft here. John had become quite adept at shaping his foxhole and soon, apart from dampness, it was reasonably habitable. He had hardly finished when he heard something in the distance, a distinct sound of heavy vehicles of some kind.

Into view came Yankees hauling their giant guns nicknamed long toms, the purpose of which no doubt was to pound the other side of the river to try to ensure a safer landing for them. They were an encouraging sight. After quick salutes between the big boys there was a consultation, and GI Joe began to manoeuvre the guns into position. Nothing to do now but wait and see. John eased into his foxhole but saw no reason why he should, for as yet nothing had come their way in the shape of bullet, shell or anything else for that matter; but orders were orders.

It did not take long for the Yankees to set up the guns, and within a short time the first salvo was fired. The noise was deafening as if all hell had been let loose. John imagined the scene on the other side of the river as these big boys thundered over, absolute panic he would think. God what a din! He ducked instinctively as the guns let go. Funny, he thought, how even though you knew they were on your side, you always ducked. No reply came from over the river. He wondered how long it would take before they would be sent over. Hardly had this thought crossed his mind when John saw that some of the boys were dragging a little craft to the water's edge. Where these tiny coracles had come from was not his business – the army organised everything – all he cared about now was that the time had come to get over to the other side. What awaited them he knew not and for the moment had no time to worry about it. His instructions had been given by a corporal hurrying by and he was on his way to take his place in the assault-boat. Not a long shelling this, but the calibre of the long toms did terrific damage and John hoped that they alone were sufficient to stave off old Jerry on the other side of the water.

As silently as possible they crept to the boats. A swish and dozens of little craft made their way across the still water, every man's eyes straining to bring the other bank into view as quickly as possible. The river was not too wide and as yet nothing was being thrown at them. Excitement mounted as the men began nearing the enemy-held bank. Still nothing as the first boats landed. John's boat was almost there and now he too was stepping out. An unbearable time this, simply nothing happening, and he felt the tension all the more as if the enemy were watching them land and were about to pounce. But so far they had made no move and the boys were advancing further inland. John was not accustomed to this. Usually they bombarded you with everything they had. This was certainly not the usual thing for old Jerry, but by God he was not complaining. He was in fact most gratefully relieved about it all, it was just so uncanny.

They were pushing inland more and more and the devastation from the long toms became evident. A few shaken civilians emerged, hands above their heads, in mortal fear of these grim strangers descending upon them, and some surprised looks as they were ignored. There was no sign of any military, which was mystifying. The men began searching houses. It was only a village this, but dying from the pounding it had taken. Cattle lay lifeless; barns were ablaze; chickens were rushing everywhere; horses had to be shot, their coats still smouldering; a house of death with the whole family in it that made one feel sick – they were somebody's parents after all. What folly! What bloody tragedy!

A white flag suddenly appeared from within a barn, the bearer being a young German officer very boyish in appearance, not the monocled type from the cinema. He began to wave the flag frantically as though afraid that he had not been spotted. He had no worries on this score. An assortment of weapons had him in their sights at once. He stepped out of the barn and, head held high, began to march towards them, his eyes searching for a show of rank. Logie moved towards him. Both men came to a halt a few paces from each other. A quick clicking of heels by the German and a form of salute by Logie. An interpreter babbled at Logie's side; the German replied; an enquiring look from Logie at the interpreter and an answer was given. More questions, more replies and then the two officers seemed to have reached an agreement on whatever they were discussing. Together with the interpreter they marched off into what John still termed enemy-held territory. If this was a trick, Logie was certainly taking chances with no escort but an interpreter. But in this man there had always been a brand of courage and judgement all of his own.

The waiting men began to get restless as half an hour passed and then before them a column began appearing. Hundreds of field grey uniforms – a seemingly endless column of glum Wehrmacht soldiers – and at the head Logie and the young German. They looked nothing like the conquering eagles of Europe now. Why was this ragged band giving up so easily? Surely there were other reasons behind this mass surrender than the mere shelling of guns? Was this one of the first signs of a crack in the morale of this once mighty force? Were these the first leaves falling off a tree as autumn appeared? How different from what they had imagined. No gloomy gory deaths, no scramble to cling to one's life – an absolute bloodless victory. What luck!

John eyed the column as it passed by him: short ones, long ones, all shapes, caps at rakish angles, both sides looking at each other as if they were from different planets. For these men the war was over. Did they feel grateful, or was the warring lust too deeply embedded? The way they looked now, they were certainly no supermen. A group of officers were bringing up the rear. These men had an air of authority about them and looked as though they found this a most distasteful affair. They glanced neither right nor left, but kept their eyes straight ahead. Cold men with a ramrod bearing; stern, unbending men. Looking at them, John felt glad that they were not issuing orders to him. He was thankful that his own officers had justice to temper their decisions, that humanity was registered in their bodies; but these cold-eyed robots seemed only to register dismay at failing in some dedicated task they had been allotted. There was a sinister air about them that was tangible as they marched past. Above their heads it seemed as if a million Jews pointed accusing fingers, children cried, mothers wept and fathers pleaded, but all in vain. John was glad when they had gone and the air felt fresher at their passing.

Epilogue

The next few weeks saw skirmishing on a small scale – nothing decisive, with the odd stubborn pocket of resistance. The prisoners were coming in ever-increasing batches. There was no doubt now that Germany was collapsing, and in their hearts the boys felt a gladness and relief that could not be described in mere words; a sense of knowing that shortly normality would return, that killing would cease and that perhaps one could begin living again. Pictures of home – wives, children, sweethearts, pints at the local, football – were in everyone's minds. But these thoughts must be discarded for it was not a certainty then, just a feeling; but at least it was there.

More villages and more towns fell as they began an almost contemptuous advance. It was getting so easy now, and resistance was being treated with surprise. The end must be in sight, for it seemed as if they had captured the whole German army just judging from the number of prisoners being taken daily. From scraps of confused news, negotiations among the top brass were in the offing. The whole German army was in a sorry state and were constantly retreating on all fronts, the morale of German prisoners was at its lowest and Montgomery was in a position of victory. The Yanks had also battered their way through and inevitably the end had come. The last shots were fired and it was over.

John's regiment had not been there long and it was all over. For John it seemed as though it were a dream; he could not grasp the full meaning of it. Does one scream, thank God, cry, laugh or become numb? His only reaction was to grab the hands of the soldier beside him and shake it vigorously. Such an insignificant gesture, and yet to John it was the only way he could think of to express his joy at the time. Some of the boys turned cartwheels, others had the temerity to slap officers on their backs and some hugged each other. It was all so sudden it was unbelievable. There would be the inevitable victory parades, the plaudits from neutral nations, the sour grapes of defeat for the vanquished; big business would pick the bones of the dead carcass, medals would be struck, blood money would be issued by bowler-hatted civil servants, and a host of other trivia would be sorted out. But what about George and Jack and Joe; Charlie and Tom? What reward for an average of 25 years of living and now six feet under, wrapped in an old mouldy army blanket marked 'Army issue, for the use of.' In the cinemas there would be empty spaces; in the locals there would be the ghosts of Billy, Jim and Joe. Football would no more echo to the voices of Charlie, Fred and Tom; wives would look at photos and children would say proudly: "That was my dad."' Altogether, life would not be the same again.

As John shook hands he felt like crying, but emotions of this kind are sometimes looked upon as a weakness, and one bottles them up even if the truth is revealed in the outburst, so grin like a machine, soldier, push back your tears John, you have won.

It is time for laughter now, no time for gloomy thoughts; no more swearing the oath to your country, your king and all his heirs and successors, onward Christian soldiers, the vicars clasp their hands for you, the women weep in gratitude, the wealthy sigh with relief, the coward ceases

trembling, the clap-trap of peace is about to be spoken –
for how long no one knows. Until angry politicians hurl
abuse across another table? How long before the dust is
brushed off another cannon, before the roar of aircraft of
a more devastating power is heard as it flies overhead
again? How many more Georges will find their way six feet
under before real peace is achieved?

You're lucky my friend John, the web of death passed you
by... this time.

RIP

CPSIA information can be obtained at www.ICGtesting.com
Printed in the USA
BVOW02s2013201213

339737BV00001B/4/P